Why this message is urgent

Jesus said to Saint Faustina

"YOU will prepare the world for the final coming." *(Diary 429)*

THIS SACRED IMAGE

O Eternal Love, You commanded Your Sacred Image to be painted, to reveal to us the inconceivable fount of your mercy. You bless whoever approaches Your rays, and a soul all black will turn to snow.

O sweet Jesus, it is here You have established the throne of your mercy to bring joy and hope to sinful man. From Your open heart, as from a pure fount flows comfort to a repentant heart and soul.

May praise and glory for this Image never cease to stream from man's soul. May the praise of God's mercy pour from every heart, now, and at every hour, and forever and ever.

O my God, when I look into the future, I am frightened, but why plunge into the future? Only the present moment is precious to me, as the future may never enter my soul at all.

It is no longer in my power, to change, correct or add to the past; for neither sages nor prophets could do that, and so, what the past has embraced I must entrust to God.

O present moment, You belong to me, whole and entire. I desire to use you as best I can, and although I am weak and small, you grant me the grace of your omnipotence.

And so, trusting in Your mercy, I will walk though life like a little child, offering You each day this heart, burning with love for Your greater glory.

Jesus I Trust in You

HANDBOOK OF DEVOTION
TO THE DIVINE MERCY

From Revelations given to

SAINT FAUSTINA

1905 - 1938

by Jesus, The Divine Mercy

Imprimi Potest	**Nihil Obstat**
+ Desmond Connell	Stephen Greene
Archbishop of Dublin	Censor Theol. Deput.
Ireland	Ireland

Feast of the Transfiguration 1994
Written and Published by Val Conlon

Ireland: Divine Mercy Publications Ireland K34 NW54
Maryville, Skerries, Co. Dublin, Ireland
Tel: 00 353 1 8491458 Fax: 00 353 1 8492466

USA: Springtime Productions Distributors
5124 Karen Dr, Fort Worth, TX 76180, **USA**
Ph: 682-557-3976

Canada: Divine Mercy Distribution Canada
2491 Dalhousie Conc. #2, R.R. #4, Lanark, ON,
KOG 1KO, Canada Tel: 613-205-1540 / 800-461-9254

Australia: Distributor wanted for this book

The sale of this book has allowed our charity to spend
millions on works of mercy over the last 25 years

our Charity is : 'Help Us Dry The Tears Foundation'
or **Divine Mercy in Action** - www.hudt.org
Contact Email: valconlon@divinemercy.org

TABLE OF CONTENTS

REASON FOR DEVOTION TO
DIVINE MERCY **NOW**

Jesus said: **If they will not adore My mercy, they will perish for all eternity. Secretary of My mercy, write, tell souls about this great mercy of Mine, because that awful day, the day of My justice, is near.**

(Diary 965)

RECOGNISE MY MERCY **NOW**
WHILE THERE IS STILL TIME

Jesus said:- **"Write down these words, my daughter. Speak to the world about My Mercy; let all mankind recognise My unfathomable mercy. It is a sign for the end times; after it, will come the day of justice. While there is still time, let them have recourse to the fount of My mercy; let them profit from the blood and water which gushed forth for them on the Cross.**

(Diary 848)

TO PEOPLE WHO SPREAD
DEVOTION TO DIVINE MERCY

Jesus said: **"Souls who spread the honour of My mercy I shield through their entire life and at the hour of death I will not be a Judge for them, but their Merciful Saviour"**,

(Diary 1075)

Saint Faustina said: **"That beautiful soul who is spreading this work of Divine Mercy throughout the world is by their deep humility, very pleasing to God"**.

(Diary 1083)

TO PRIESTS WHO SPREAD
DEVOTION TO DIVINE MERCY

Jesus said, **"Tell my priests that hardened sinners will crumble beneath their words when they speak about My unfathomable mercy, about the compassion I have for them in My Heart. To priests who will proclaim and extol My mercy I will give wonderful power, and I will anoint their words and I will touch the hearts of those to which they will speak"**.

(Diary 1521)

THE FOUNDATION OF DEVOTION TO DIVINE MERCY

IS TRUST

Jesus said: **The Graces of My Mercy are drawn by means of one vessel only, that is TRUST. The more a soul trusts the more it will receive.** *(Diary 1578)*

Sooner would Heaven and Earth turn into nothingness than would My Mercy not embrace a trusting soul. *(Diary 1777)*

MERCY

Jesus said: **You are to be my living reflection through love and mercy, be always merciful toward other people, especially toward sinners.** *(Diary 1446)*

Love everyone out of Love for Me.
(Diary 1695)

TELL THE WORLD OF MY MERCY

The message of Divine Mercy is at the heart of the gospel. It presents the truth and the call of the gospel and was proclaimed by St. Pope John Paul II, in his encyclical Rich in Mercy, as a message from God for our time.

The Church must consider it one of her principal duties - at every stage of history and especially in our modern age - to proclaim and to introduce into life, the mystery of God's Divine Mercy, supremely revealed in Jesus Christ on the Cross.

Over and over again Our Lord expressed His desire to Saint Faustina that the whole world be convinced of His mercy, and He promised to defend throughout their lives those who would proclaim His mercy.

JESUS IS SAYING TO **YOU**

Proclaim to the whole world My unfathomable mercy. Do not be discouraged by the difficulties you encounter in proclaiming My mercy. These difficulties that affect you so painfully are evidence that this work is Mine.

(Diary 1142)

ST. POPE JOHN PAUL II'S ADDRESS AT
THE CANONISATION OF
ST. FAUSTINA, 30TH APRIL, 2000

John Paul II said: "Today my joy is truly great in presenting the life and witness of Sr. Faustina Kowalska to the whole Church as a gift of God for our time. By Divine Providence, the life of this humble daughter of Poland was completely linked with the history of the 20th century, the century we have just left behind. In fact, it was between the First and Second World Wars that Christ entrusted his message of mercy to her. Those who remember, who were witnesses and participants in the events of those years and the horrible sufferings they caused for millions of people, know well how necessary was this message of mercy. Jesus told Sr.

Faustina: "Humanity will not find peace until it turns trustfully to Divine Mercy" (Diary, 132).

Sr. Faustina's canonisation has a particular eloquence; **and by this act today, I intend to pass this message on to the new millennium.** *I pass it on to all people, so that they will learn to know ever better the face of God and the true face of their brethren. What will the years ahead bring us? What will man's future on earth be like? We are not given to know. However, it is certain that in addition to new progress there will unfortunately be no lack of painful experiences. But the light of Divine Mercy, which the Lord in a way wished to return to the world through Sr. Faustina's charism, will light the way for the men and women of the third millennium.*

As the Apostles once did, today too, humanity must welcome into the upper room of history, the risen Christ, who shows the wounds of his Crucifixion and repeats: Peace be with you! Humanity must let itself be touched and pervaded by the Spirit given to it by the risen Christ. It is the Spirit who heals the wounds of the heart, pulls down the barriers that separate us from God and divide us from one another, and at the same time, restores the joy of the Father's love, and of fraternal unity. Love of God and love of neighbour are inseparable.

BE APOSTLES OF DIVINE MERCY!

This was the appeal of St. Pope John Paul II in his homily when he celebrated the Feast of Mercy at "Santo Spirito in Sassia" a beautiful little Church not far from St. Peter's and where there is a spiritual centre of Divine Mercy.

The Pope in his homily said: "The mystical experience of Sr. Faustina and her cry to the merciful Christ belong to the harsh context of our century. As people of this century, we would like to thank the Lord for the message of Divine Mercy."

Contemporary civilisation does all it can to distract human attention from the inescapable reality of death, and tries to induce man to live as though death did not exist, and this is expressed particularly in the attempt to turn man's conscience away from God.

The Pope finished by saying "I would like to say to all, **trust in the Lord, be apostles of Divine Mercy** and follow the invitation and example of Sr. Faustina...Give thanks to the Lord, for he is good, for his Mercy endures for ever."

From L'Osservatore Romano, Vatican City, 3rd May, 1995

Pope John Paul II blesses the Divine Image at 3 o'clock on the Feast of Mercy

Saint Faustina

"You are the secretary of My Mercy, I have chosen you for that office in this life and in the next."

(Diary 1605).

Helena Kowalska was born on August 25, 1905, in the village of Glogowiec, in Poland. She was the third of ten children. Her parents were poor but they taught their children the love of God, and respect for other people. Her whole life was characterised by those virtues. When she was twenty years old, she entered the apostolic congregation of the Sisters of Our Lady of Mercy, where as a humble and hard-working sister, she lived the final thirteen years of her short life. Fervent love of God and all humanity, led her to the summit of self-sacrifice and heroism. She distinguished herself by a special devotion to Jesus with great trust in His Divine Mercy which she endeavoured to instill into everyone who came to know her.

She died in the odour of sanctity on October 5th, 1938, in the convent of her congregation at Lagiewniki in Cracow, Poland, and was buried there in her community's cemetery. During the informative process of her beatification, her remains were transferred from the cemetery to the convent chapel, where they now lie in a reliquary at the side altar. The remains may in time be moved to a final resting place in the new basilica now complete, beside the convent.

SHORT HISTORY OF THE
DEVOTION TO THE DIVINE MERCY

On February 22, 1931, Sister Faustina records in her Diary "I saw Jesus dressed in a white garment. He held one hand raised in blessing and the other hand was touching his garment at the breast. From under the garment came two rays of light, one red the other pale".

Jesus said **"paint a picture according to the vision you see, with the signature, Jesus, I trust in You, I desire that this picture be venerated first in your chapel and then throughout the whole world"**. Later Sr. Faustina's Spiritual Director told her to ask Jesus what the rays signified and Jesus explained to her:

The rays represent the Blood and Water which gushed forth from the depths of my Mercy when My agonising Heart was pierced on the cross. The pale rays symbolise the water, which cleanses and purifies the soul: the red rays represent the blood, which gives new life to the soul. These rays will shield the soul before the justice of My Father. Fortunate are those who live in this shelter, for the justice of God will not reach them there".

St. Faustina writes in her diary: "The Lord permitted me to see the immensity and greatness of His Mercy. If souls could only realise how much God loves them! Earthly human understanding, is only a pale shadow of the reality," Jesus pleaded for help in seeking the return, through His mercy, of all who have lost their faith and offended God.

Write, the greater the sinner, the greater the mercy. Summon all those to confidence in the incomprehensible depth of My Mercy for I desire to save all. The well of Mercy was opened wide with a lance on the Cross, for all souls. I do not exclude anyone."

Again and again, Our Lord visited Sister Faustina and repeated His appeal to sinners calling them to His open arms. **"Know, my daughter, that My Heart is Mercy itself. From this sea of mercy graces pour out upon the whole world. No souls that come to Me depart without being comforted. All misery vanishes in My Mercy: and every grace, redemptive and sanctifying, stems from this source".**

On another occasion, Jesus complained of our lack of trust in Him **"Distrust tears at My Heart. The lack of confidence in chosen souls hurts Me most. Despite My inexhaustible love, they do not trust Me.**

Tell ailing mankind to draw close to My Merciful Heart and I will fill them with peace. Mankind will not find solace until it turns with confidence to My Mercy and love."

THE DIVINE IMAGE AND THE PROMISE

Our Lord instructed Saint Faustina to paint His Image with the signature **"Jesus I trust in You"**. Our Lord wished the Image of His resurrection to be venerated and attached a great promise to it:

I promise that the soul that will venerate this image will not perish. I further promise to that soul victory over enemies here on earth especially at the hour of death. I Myself, shall defend that soul as My own glory..."

THE SIGNATURE

There is considered opinion that Jesus meant each of us to personally sign this Image, **"Jesus I trust in You"**. (*This would suffice on back of Image Picture*)

HISTORY OF THE CHAPLET OF MERCY

On September 13, 1935, Sister Faustina saw an angel, depicted to her as the executor of God's wrath. She saw the angel about to visit a certain city on earth and carry out punishment on its sinful inhabitants. She was sad, she prayed hard and begged the angel for mercy, but somehow she realised that her prayers were without power to appease the wrath of God in this instance. Then suddenly the Holy Trinity was manifested before her, and she heard these words:

Eternal Father, I offer you the Body and Blood, Soul and Divinity of Your dearly beloved Son, Our Lord Jesus Christ in atonement for our sins and those of the whole world". This prayer, as part of the full chaplet of Divine Mercy had the exceptional power to have the chastisement stopped. Jesus explained to Saint Faustina how He wished this prayer said. *(It can be said on ordinary rosary beads.)*

Jesus said: "Say unceasingly this chaplet. Anyone who says it will receive great mercy at the hour of death. Priests will recommend it to sinners as a last hope. If the most hardened sinner recites this chaplet even once, they will receive grace from My infinite Mercy. I want the whole world to know My infinite Mercy. I want to give unimaginable graces to those who trust in My Mercy".

THE NOVENA FOR SISTER FAUSTINA

Our blessed Lord also gave Sister Faustina (for herself alone, see page 47), a Novena to His Mercy. She was to start it on Good Friday, that wonderful day when Christ first revealed how merciful and loving He was, by His Sacrifice on the Cross. Saint Faustina wrote in her diary that she began the novena for the conversion of the whole world, that all may recognise God's Mercy and that all souls may speak of His Goodness.

Jesus said: **"I desire the confidence of My people. Let not even the weak and very sinful fear to approach me: even if their sins be as numerous as all the sands of the earth all will be forgiven in the fathomless pit of My Mercy."**

During these nine days I want you to lead souls to the Fount of My Mercy, in order that they may draw from it strength, refreshment, and all the graces they need in the trials of their lives, especially at the hour of death. Each day you will lead a different group of souls and immerse them in the sea of My Mercy. Each day you will beseech the Father through My bitter Passion, for graces for these souls."

She received all the instructions on how to make this novena which begins on page 51.

The novena of Chaplets can be made at any time, but Our Lord especially wished that it be made beginning Good Friday in preparation for the Feast of His Mercy, which should be celebrated on the first Sunday after Easter.

My daughter, speak to the world of My inexhaustible Mercy. I desire that this feast be a refuge and a shelter for all souls, especially for poor sinners. The very depths of My Mercy will be opened on that day. I will pour out a sea of graces upon those souls that will approach the fount of My Mercy on this day."

The souls that will go to confession in preparation, and Communion on the day will obtain a complete remission of all sin and all punishment. (Try to make it on the Sunday of the Feast, but if not possible, make it as close to the Sunday as possible). The important condition is that your soul is in grace.

"Let no soul fear to come to Me, even if its sins be as scarlet. This feast emerged from the bosom of My Mercy and is founded in the depths of My Mercies. I desire that it be celebrated with great solemnity on the first Sunday after Easter". *See footnote page 29*

According to this great promise, Jesus is offering all souls a chance for a new "baptism" each year, giving everyone an opportunity to "wipe the soul clean". If a soul, taking advantage of this great gift in all sincerity and with proper contrition, was to die after receiving Holy Communion on the Feast of Mercy and before committing another sin, they would go immediately to Heaven, **without anytime in Purgatory - regardless of past life.** There seems to be no other meaning to this promise of Our Lord. This is the unbelievable and little understood love and mercy of God for sinners.

On the canonisation of Sr. Faustina, 30th April 2000, Pope John Paul II instituted this feast in the church. In future the Sunday after Easter will be known as Mercy Sunday.

Exhorting people to hasten to Him before it is too late, Jesus said: **"before I come as the just one, I first open wide the gates of My Mercy. He who does not pass through the gates of my Mercy must pass through the gates of justice."**

Jesus permitted her to see the enormity of people's sins on earth. She was frightened at their hideousness, and asked Jesus how He could suffer such terrible insult. Jesus told her, concerning the many terrible sins committed in the world. **"I have eternity for the punishment of these. For now I prolong my Mercy. But, woe to him who ignores the time of My Mercy."**

Another time He said: **"My daughter, the flames of My Mercy burn bright. I desire to pour it out on human souls. Oh what pain they cause Me when they do not accept it."**

PROCLAIM HIS MERCY

Our Blessed Mother often appeared to Saint Faustina too. On the Feast of the Annunciation in 1936, Mary said to her: **"I gave the world a Saviour, You must make known His Mercy, and prepare the world for His Second Coming. He will then come, not as a Merciful Saviour, but as a just Judge. Oh how terrible is that day! Determined is the day of justice. Angels tremble before it. Speak to souls of His great Mercy while there is still time. If you remain silent now, you will have to account for a great number of souls on that final day. Fear nothing. Be faithful to the end."**

Now it is up to all of us to tell the world about the love and mercy of God. Our Saviour left a promise for those who would become apostles of His message. He said to Saint Faustina: **"I protect, as a mother does a child, the souls that promote devotion to My Mercy during their lifetime; and in the hour of their death, I will not be their judge, but their Saviour. In that final hour the soul does not have anything in its defence save My Mercy, for justice will not reach it there. Speak to the whole world of My Mercy and love. Let it know how incomprehensible it is. It is a sign of the approaching last days, after which the day of justice will come. While there is still time let them take refuge in the fount of My Mercy."**

SUBSEQUENT HISTORY

One day in 1935, Saint Faustina wrote for her spiritual director: "The time will come when this work, which God so commends, will be as though in complete ruin, and suddenly the action of God will come upon the scene with real power which will bear witness to the truth. It will be as a new splendour for the church, though it had for some time been dormant in it."

This indeed came to pass. On the 6th of March 1959, the Holy See, acting on information that was inaccurately presented, prohibited the spreading of images and writings advocating devotion to the Divine Mercy in the form proposed by Sister Faustina. As a result, there followed almost twenty years of suppression of the message.

ACCEPTANCE BY THE CHURCH

On the 15th April, 1978, the Holy See, after a thorough examination of original documents previously unavailable to it, completely reversed its decision and permitted the spread of this devotion.

The man primarily responsible for reversal of this decision was Karol Wojtyla, the Archbishop of Saint Faustina's home diocese of Cracow. On October 16th 1978, he was elevated to the See of St. Peter as Pope John Paul II.

THE FEAST OF MERCY
(A Second Baptism)

This following article is from a lecture by Canon Ignacy Rozycki Prelate of Honour of his Holiness, Doctor of Dogmatic Theology, former Professor of Theology at the Jagiellonian University, Professor of Theology at the Pontifical Theological Academy in Cracow, Poland, and a member of the International Theological Commission. He said "Among the external manifestations of the Devotion to The Divine Mercy **the Feast of Mercy occupies the first place".** The Lord Jesus made known His will (*about this feast*) already in the opening revelation concerning this devotion (on February 22, 1931). For the establishment of this Feast, He devoted fourteen revelations. Of Saint Faustina He required that the feast be preceded by a novena of Chaplets to the Divine Mercy. Jesus also personally dictated to her a very beautiful novena intended however, primarily for her own use. He attached such importance to this feast that in the 43rd revelation He stated: **"My Heart rejoices on account of this Feast."** (*Diary 998*)

The Feast of Mercy is to be celebrated on the First Sunday after Easter. *The selection of this Sunday, as well as the distinct desire of Jesus that priests preach sermons on this day about Divine Mercy, especially that mercy which God bestows upon us through Christ,* all serve to indicate that Jesus sees a strict connection between the paschal mystery of our redemption and this feast: it is designed for the purpose that we contemplate on that day the mystery of Redemption as the greatest revelation of Divine Mercy towards us. Saint Faustina also took note of the connection between the Feast of Mercy and the mystery of the Redemption when in 1935 she wrote: *"I see now that the work of Redemption is bound up with the work of Mercy that the Lord desires."* (Diary 89)

Jesus asks that the Feast of Mercy be preceded by a Novena. From Sister Faustina He required a preparation for its observance by means of a **novena consisting of the recitation of the Chaplet of the Divine Mercy**. He gave her orders to set down in writing, and in part He dictated to her, another novena that is inserted in the third notebook of her Diary. It is beautiful and profound **but intended for her own use only**. But the novena consisting of the recitation of the **Chaplet of Mercy and intended for use by the whole world** unites within itself the promises of Jesus, on the one hand, to the recitation of this chaplet, and, on the other hand, to the making of the novena (of chaplets) before the Feast of Mercy. Concerning this novena Jesus said. **"By this (the Chaplet) novena I will grant souls all possible graces"** *(Diary 796)*. The words "all possible graces" mean that people making this novena to the Divine Mercy will obtain every sort of divine blessing they ask for regardless of whether they pray for graces for themselves **or for others.**

Jesus demands that the feast be celebrated solemnly, that is, as a liturgical feast of the Church Universal. *With regard to the manner of its celebration He expressed two wishes: in the first place, the image of the Divine Mercy is to be ceremoniously blessed on this feast, and on this same Sunday it is to be publicly, that is, liturgically venerated (Diary 341 see also 47-50 and 88).* Secondly, **"On that day priests are to speak to souls about this great and unfathomable Mercy of Mine."** *(Diary 570)*

Jesus requires then, that the subject of sermons on that day be on His mercy, not only His divine and infinite mercy, but also the unimaginable mercy of His human heart, the evidence of which is, above all, His Passion, for he wants *"that the Feast of Mercy be a refuge and shelter for all souls, and especially for poor sinners."* Since there is no other means of drawing graces from the well spring of Mercy but through *trust*, the sermon should be of the sort that it be capable of stirring up in the hearers an unwavering and fervent attitude of *trust in Jesus*.

The preacher will be able to do justice to this assignment only if he manages to show the faithful the inconceivable love and mercy of Jesus both in His Passion and in the entire work of the Redemption. Thus, the going quickly through the whole work of Redemption from the point of view of the Redemption is the special purpose of this feast. In sermons preached on this day it is proper also by all means to direct attention to the most singular grace which Jesus attached to the celebration of this feast. Namely,

"The soul that will go to confession and receive Holy Communion shall obtain complete forgiveness of sins and punishment"

(Diary 699).

Our Lord does not explicitly say we have to get confession on the Feast itself.

(Diary 299-301, 699)

Note: *Sr. Faustina herself made it on the Saturday before the feast.* *(Diary 1072)*

This extraordinary grace promised by Jesus in connection with the Feast of Mercy is something greater by far than a plenary indulgence. A plenary indulgence consists only in the forgiveness of temporal punishment due to sins already forgiven, it is never the forgiveness of sins themselves.

The remarkable grace of the Feast of Mercy is also very much akin to the grace of Baptism. The Sacramental grace of Baptism received by an adult is not only the removal of original sin but is also the forgiveness of all personal sins and any punishment due to them so the soul cleansed on the Feast of Mercy is like the soul of one newly baptised in the promises mentioned, however, Christ joined the forgiveness of all sins and punishment to the Holy Communion received on the Feast of Mercy. **In other words so far as that matter is concerned He raised it (the Holy Communion on the Feast of Mercy) to the rank of a second Baptism."**

It is obvious that in order to effect the complete forgiveness of sin and punishment the Holy Communion on the Feast of Mercy must not only be a worthy one, but in fact, must also be the expression of the fulfilment of the basic requirement of the Divine Mercy Devotion.

Unworthily received, or not accompanied by complete trust in the Divine Mercy and by carrying out a deed of mercy as preparation for the feast, it would be a contradiction of Devotion to the Divine Mercy. It is also your duty to tell others about the great grace they can receive on this day. Otherwise instead of the most singular grace, it could draw divine wrath upon the head of the recipient.

The spiritual good of the faithful demands that they know what great graces they can obtain by the Holy Communion received on the Feast of Mercy, and under what conditions they can obtain them. Jesus did not limit His generosity on the Feast of Mercy exclusively to this most extraordinary grace. On the contrary, Jesus declared that "on that day the very depths of My tender mercy are open; I pour out a whole ocean of graces upon those souls who will approach the fount of My mercy. On that day all the divine floodgates through which graces flow are opened."

Therefore, let no soul fear to draw near to Me, even though its sins be as scarlet," (Diary 699). From these words of Christ it is evident that he fervently desires the Feast of Mercy to be an unusually effective refuge for all people, especially sinners incomparably more effective than all the other forms of Devotion to the Divine Mercy. The incomparable effectiveness of this refuge is manifested in three ways:

Firstly, through its universality, all people, even those who hitherto never had devotion to the Divine Mercy **(even sinners who repent on the day of the Feast itself)** can participate to the fullest extent in all the graces which Jesus prepared for this feast.

Secondly, on this day Jesus not only wishes to shower people with saving graces for eternal life, but also with temporal blessings for this life; and this refers both to individuals as well as to communities of people, since He said: **"Mankind will have no peace until it turns** *(as to a source of help)* **to the fount of My mercy"** *(Diary 699)*

Thirdly, all graces and benefits, even in their highest degrees, are this day accessible to everyone so long as they are asked for with great trust. Christ did not attach such an extraordinary abundance of benefits and graces to any other form of devotion.

(Analysis by Canon Ignacy Rozycki, Doctor of Dogmatic Theology. Appointed by John Paul II for this purpose.)

WHAT JESUS ASKS OF US FOR
HIS FEAST OF MERCY

Canon Ignacy Rozycki, Doctor of Dogmatic Theology appointed by Pope John Paul II to examine the revelations to Saint Faustina, came to the conclusion that the extraordinary grace promised by Jesus on the Feast of Mercy is a gift of grace equalled only by the grace of Holy Baptism. This means that on this day your soul can be renewed as on the day of baptism, after receiving this grace on the feast day, you then only have to worry about the sins you commit in the future, your past life and sins no longer exist.

The Feast of Mercy is now officially celebrated on the Sunday after Easter, as requested by our Lord. *(Diary 280, 299-301)*

The Feast should be preceded by a Novena of Chaplets to the Divine Mercy beginning on Good Friday. You may of course say the other novena as well but it was for St. Faustina only.

The Sermon by the priest on that day should be on Divine Mercy - that is the mercy which God the Father bestows on us through Jesus Christ His son. *(Diary 570)*

That we contemplate, on this day, the Mystery of Redemption as the greatest revelation of Divine Mercy towards us. *(Diary 299-301)*

The Image of the Divine Mercy is to be ceremoniously blessed on the day. (Diary 47-341)

The Image is to be publicly venerated. The image should be exposed to all taking part in the celebration (to demonstrate this, an image could be left in a position that all can touch and say "Jesus I Trust In You"). *This can be carried out during the celebration like the kissing of the cross on Good Friday or as people leave the Church, if numbers prevent it during the ceremony.* (Diary 341-570-742)

Confession and communion on the day. If confession is not available on the day it should be as close to the day as possible. St. Faustina made it on the Saturday before the Feast. Communion, as always, should be a worthy one and must be accompanied by complete Trust in Divine Mercy. (Diary 699 - 1109) *It's important your soul be in grace.*

That an act of Mercy should take place in our lives, as part of our preparation for the feast. We should be merciful to others in our words, deeds and prayers.

Merciful Word *Forgiving and comforting*
Merciful Deed *Any of the corporal works of mercy*
Merciful Prayer *Prayers for Mercy for the world*

BLESSING FOR THE IMAGE ON
THE FEAST OF MERCY

V. Our help is in the name of the Lord.
R. Who made heaven and earth.
V. The Lord be with you.
R. And also with you.

Let us Pray;

Almighty, Eternal God, You have allowed pictures and statues of Your Saints to be painted and carved, so that as often as we look upon them with our bodily eyes, we may recall with our more inward eyes their deeds and their sanctity and learn to imitate them. In Your goodness, therefore, bless and sanctify, this picture fashioned to reveal to us the unfathomable love of our Crucified and Risen Saviour - *Divine Mercy Personified* - and to recall to our minds the streams of Blood and Water gushing forth from His pierced heart to be a fount of mercy for us. **Grant to all who invoke Your Mercy with this picture before their eyes, the grace of true repentance, pardon and peace. Shield them from every danger to soul and body**.

Loving Saviour, establish in this picture the *Throne of Your Mercy.* Pour out upon all who approach it with faith and trust, the purifying, healing and sanctifying rays of grace ever emanating from it as from a blazing sun. Gaze upon them from it as You did from the Cross with irresistible love and compassion.

Through this Image may Your Divine Mercy triumph over all the powers and wiles of Satan the world over. May all who venerate it never perish. May it be their joy in life, their hope in death and their glory in eternity. This we ask through Christ Our Lord. Amen.

With Ecclesiastical Permission: Desmond, 12th March, 1991. His Grace the Most Reverend, Desmond Connell, D.D., Archbishop of Dublin.

THE MERCY OF GOD IN THE GOSPEL

It was to announce His unconditional love for man that God chose the human road. This is in fact the good news brought by Jesus: the encounter of Divine Love with our misery, our sick humanity. He is a "Samaritan" God who comes from afar, who comes close and comforts the dying (each one of us is the entire mankind) he embraces him, washes and cleanses his wounds, cares for him with the oil of His love, and cures him forever (*Luke 10.30-35*). He is the "shepherd" God who searches for the lost sheep (*Matthew 9.36*) and who, after leaving the other ninety nine in the hills and in the desert, goes in search of the one lost sheep (*Luke 15.4-7*). He is also the "healing" God who comes to seek out and cure those in need, the sinners. **(*Mark 2 - 17*).**

He is the "father" who awaits anxiously the Son who has left home and on his return runs to him, embraces him and prepares a great feast (*Luke 15.11-24*)

Jesus himself claims to have been chosen to bring the good news to the poor, to proclaim liberty to the captives, and recovery of sight to the blind, to set free the oppressed and to announce that the time has come when the Lord will save his people (*Luke 4.18-19*) and he gives witness of his works saying "Go and tell John what you have seen and heard, the blind can see, the lame can walk, those who suffer from dreaded skin diseases are made clean, the deaf can hear, the dead are raised to life, and the good news is preached to the poor." (*Luke 7.22*)

THE FIRST DIVINE MERCY IMAGE

The DIVINE MERCY IMAGE first appeared to Sister Faustina in her room on 22nd February 1931. *"In the evening in my cell, I saw Jesus clothed in white, one hand raised in blessing the other resting on His breast. From His garment came rays of light, one red and the other pale in colour. Jesus said to me,*

"Paint an Image according to the vision you see, with the signature "Jesus I trust in You."

I desire that this Image be venerated first in your chapel and then throughout the world. The two beams of light shining forth from My Heart are the symbols of blood and water that poured from My side on the day of My Sacrifice on Calvary.

The pale beam represents the water that cleanses and purifies souls, the red, the blood that gives new life to souls".

THE PROPHECY (I.35)

Write this down, that before My coming as judge I shall come first as the King of Mercy. Before the coming of that day of justice, there will be a sign in the heavens. All light will be extinguished in heaven and earth. There will appear in the sky the Sign of the Cross. From each of the wounds on My hands and feet will shine forth a light that will for a brief time brighten the earth. This will be a short time before the last day."

Jesus I Trust in You

"BE MERCIFUL EVEN AS YOUR
FATHER IS MERCIFUL"

(Luke 6:36)

Jesus Christ taught that man not only receives and experiences the mercy of God, but that he is also called to practice mercy towards others, "Blessed are the merciful for they shall obtain mercy" *(Mt 5:7)*

The Church sees in these words a call to action, and tries to practise mercy. Man attains to the merciful love of God His mercy, to the extent that he himself is interiorly transformed in the spirit of that love towards his neighbour."

(John Paul II, *Rich in Mercy*, 14)

DEEDS OF MERCY

The revelations given to Saint Faustina confirm this, in that they include the need of practising mercy towards one's neighbour **daily:** ... by deed, word, or prayer, *(Diary 1313)* as a second foundation stone ... **If a soul does not exercise mercy in some way or other it will not obtain My mercy on judgement day. Oh, if only souls knew how to gather eternal treasure for themselves, they would not be** judged, because even the strongest faith is of no avail without works (of mercy), for they would forestall my judgement with mercy *(Diary 1317)*.

One of the purposes for which Our Lord ordered Saint Faustina to paint a special image of Himself as Divine Mercy, was as Jesus said... **to be a reminder of the demands of My Mercy.** *(Diary 742)*.

Trust in Jesus and extending mercy toward other people are the very soul of this devotion, and works of mercy are part of a long tradition of genuine Christian living.

(see page 132)

The Church teaches us to be merciful in various ways:

THE CORPORAL WORKS OF MERCY

1. Feed the hungry.
2. Give drink to the thirsty.
3. Clothe the naked.
4. Shelter the homeless,
5. Comfort the imprisoned.
6. Visit the sick.
7. Bury the dead.

THE SPIRITUAL WORKS OF MERCY

1. Admonish sinners.
2. Instruct the uninformed.
3. Counsel the doubtful.
4. Comfort the sorrowful.
5. Be patient with those in error.
6. Forgive offenses.
7. Pray for the living and the dead.

PRAYERS
FROM THE DIARY
OF
SAINT FAUSTINA

GRACES RECEIVED BY RECITATION
OF THE CHAPLET OF DIVINE MERCY

Our Lord said to the servant of God, Saint Faustina: **"Unceasingly recite this chaplet that I have taught you. Whoever will recite it will receive great mercy at the hour of death... priests will recommend it to sinners as a last hope of salvation. Even the most hardened sinner, if he recites this chaplet even once, will receive grace from My infinite mercy.** *(Diary 687)* ... **Oh, what great graces I will grant souls who will recite this chaplet** *(Diary 848)*...**By means of it you can ask and obtain anything, if what you ask for will be compatible with My will** *(Diary 1731)*...**I want the whole world to know My infinite mercy. I want to give unimaginable graces to those who trust in My mercy"**. *(Diary 687)*.

HOW TO RECITE THE CHAPLET/ROSARY

The Lord said to Saint Faustina: **You will recite this chaplet on the beads of the Rosary in the following manner:**

First of all you will say, one **OUR FATHER,** one **HAIL MARY,** and the **I BELIEVE IN GOD"**.

THE CHAPLET
SAY ONE OUR FATHER

Our Father, who art in heaven
hallowed be Thy Name;
Thy kingdom come;
Thy will be done on earth as it is in heaven.
Give us this day our daily bread;
and forgive us our trespasses
as we forgive those who trespass against us;
and lead us not into temptation
but deliver us from evil. Amen.

SAY ONE HAIL MARY

Hail Mary, full of grace.
The Lord is with Thee.
Blessed art Thou amongst women,
and blessed is the fruit of Thy womb, Jesus.
Holy Mary, Mother of God,
pray for us sinners,
now, and at the hour of our death. Amen.

THE APOSTLE'S CREED

I believe in God the Father Almighty, Creator of Heaven and Earth, and in Jesus Christ His only Son, Our Lord, Who was conceived by the Holy Spirit, born of the Virgin Mary, suffered under Pontius Pilate, was crucified, died and was buried. He descended into Hell. The third day He rose again from the dead. He ascended into Heaven and is seated at the right hand of God the Father Almighty. From thence He shall come to judge the living and the dead. I believe in the Holy Spirit, the holy Catholic Church, the communion of Saints, the forgiveness of sins, the resurrection of the body and life everlasting. Amen.

Then on the OUR FATHER BEADS you will say the following words:

Eternal Father, I offer You the Body and Blood, Soul and Divinity of Your dearly beloved Son, Our Lord Jesus Christ, in atonement for our sins and those of the whole world.

On the HAIL MARY BEADS you will say the following words:

For the sake of His sorrowful Passion have mercy on us and on the whole world.

In conclusion after the five decades you will say three times:

Holy God, Holy Mighty One, Holy Immortal One have mercy on us and on the whole world.

(It is this Chaplet that is used as a Novena beginning on Good Friday in preparation for the Feast of Mercy.)

THE CHAPLET OF DIVINE MERCY AS A NOVENA

Sister Faustina wrote in her Diary: "The Lord told me to recite this chaplet for the nine days before the Feast of Mercy. It is to **begin on Good Friday. Then he told me: By this novena (of Chaplets) I will grant every possible grace to souls** *(Diary 796)* From this and other passages in the Diary it appears that the Lord wants us to make novenas of the Chaplet for whatever need. In preparation for the Feast of Mercy many people devoted to the Divine Mercy say the novena given to Saint Faustina for Our Lord's intentions without saying a novena of Chaplets. It is important to realise that it is the novena of Chaplets that Our Lord attached such importance to, and the promise, therefore a novena of Chaplets must be said in preparation for the Feast of Mercy.

IMPORTANCE OF THE
CHAPLET OF MERCY
FOR THE DYING

Jesus said:

Write that when they say this Chaplet in the presence of the dying, I will stand between My Father and the dying person, not as the just judge but as the merciful Saviour"

Diary of Sister Faustina (Diary 1541)

THE HOUR OF GREAT MERCY
The moment of three o'clock in the Afternoon

A devotion most dear to Our Lord is the veneration of His Passion at the very hour that recalls His death on the Cross. Throughout the passion and death of Our Lord Jesus, the very Kingdom of God was opened to us. What love should fill our hearts and how willingly we should respond to the request of Our Lord who said to Saint Faustina: "At three o'clock implore My Mercy especially for sinners; and if only for a brief moment immerse yourself in My Passion, particularly in My abandonment at the moment of agony...This is the hour of great mercy for the whole world... At this hour I will refuse nothing to the soul that makes a request of Me in virtue of My Passion. *(Diary 1320)*

I remind you, My daughter, that as often as you hear the clock strike the third hour, immerse yourself completely in My Mercy, adoring and glorifying it; invoke its omnipotence for the whole world, and particularly for poor sinners; for at that moment mercy was opened wide for every soul. At this hour you can obtain everything for yourself, and for others for the asking; it was the time of grace for the whole world - the moment that mercy triumphed over justice. *(Diary 1572)*

My daughter, try your best to make the stations of the Cross at this hour, provided that your duties permit it; and if you are not able to make the Stations of the Cross, then at least step into the chapel for a moment and adore, in the Most Blessed Sacrament, My Heart which is full of mercy, and should you be unable to step into the chapel, immerse yourself in prayer, wherever you happen to be, if only for a very brief instant".

SUGGESTED THREE O'CLOCK PRAYERS
At this hour you can obtain everything for yourself and for others

Beg Jesus, at this hour (the hour of 3 o'clock) to have mercy on all the poor souls who are about to die and are on their way to eternal damnation. No greater act of mercy, can you pray for.

You expired, Jesus, but the source of life gushed forth for souls and an ocean of mercy opened up for the whole world. O Fount of Life, unfathomable Divine Mercy, envelop the whole world and empty Yourself out upon us.

This prayer was given to Saint Faustina as a conversion prayer, (see p.62) it has been adopted as an appropriate prayer for 3 o'clock.

O Blood and Water, which gushed forth from the Heart of Jesus as a fount of mercy for us, I trust in You."

SAINT FAUSTINA'S NOVENA TO THE DIVINE MERCY*

A *Novena to The Divine Mercy which Jesus instructed me to write down and to make before the Feast of Mercy. It begins on Good Friday."*

Our Lord's words recorded by Saint Faustina:

I desire that during these nine days you bring souls to the fount of My Mercy, that they may draw strength therefrom, and refreshment and whatever graces they have need of, in the hardships of life, and especially at the hour of death.

On each day you will bring to My Heart a different group of souls and you will immerse them in this ocean of My Mercy, and I will bring all these souls into the house of My Father.

On each day you will beg My Father, on the strength of My bitter Passion, for graces for these souls."

People may of course make this Novena to the Divine Mercy but it would be secondary to the

*Novena of Chaplets which **must** be made in preparation for the Feast of Mercy.*

Saint Faustina continues: "I answered, Jesus, I do not know how to make this novena and which souls to bring first into Your Most Compassionate Heart. Jesus replied that He would tell me which souls to bring each day into His Heart." (*Diary 1209*)

FIRST DAY

TODAY BRING TO ME ALL MANKIND, ESPECIALLY ALL SINNERS, and immerse them in the ocean of My mercy. In this way you will console Me in the bitter grief into which the loss of souls plunges Me".

Most merciful Jesus, whose very nature it is to have compassion on us and to forgive us, do not look upon our sins, but upon our trust which we place in Your infinite goodness. Receive us all into the abode of Your Most Compassionate Heart, and never let us escape from it. We beg this of You by Your love which unites You to the Father and the Holy Spirit. Eternal Father, turn Your merciful gaze upon all mankind and especially upon poor sinners, all enfolded in the Most Compassionate Heart of Jesus. For the sake of His sorrowful Passion show us Your Mercy, that we may praise the infinite power of Your Mercy for ever and ever. Amen.

SECOND DAY

TODAY BRING TO ME THE SOULS OF PRIESTS AND RELIGIOUS and immerse them in My unfathomable mercy. It was they who gave Me strength to endure My bitter Passion. Through them, as through channels, My Mercy flows out upon mankind".

Most Merciful Jesus, from whom comes all that is good, increase Your grace in men and women* consecrated to your service, that they perform worthy works of mercy, and that all who see them may glorify the Father of Mercy who is in heaven. Eternal Father, turn Your merciful gaze upon the company of chosen ones in Your vineyard - upon the souls of priests and religious - and endow them with the strength of Your blessing. For the love of the Heart of Your Son in which they are enfolded, impart to them Your power and light, that they may be able to guide others in the way of salvation, and with one voice sing praise to Your boundless mercy for ages without end*. Amen.

*In the original text, Saint Faustina uses the pronoun "us" since she was offering this prayer as a consecrated religious sister. The wording adapted here is intended to make the prayer suitable for universal use.

THIRD DAY

TODAY BRING TO ME ALL DEVOUT AND FAITHFUL SOULS and immerse them in the ocean of My mercy. These souls brought Me consolation on the way of the Cross. They were that drop of consolation in the midst of an ocean of bitterness".

Most Merciful Jesus, from the treasury of Your mercy, You impart Your graces in great abundance to each and all. Receive us into the abode of Your most compassionate Heart and never let us escape from it. We beg this grace of You by that most wondrous love for the heavenly Father with which Your Heart burns so fiercely.

Eternal Father, turn Your merciful gaze upon faithful souls, as upon the inheritance of Your Son. For the sake of His sorrowful Passion grant them Your blessing and surround them with Your constant protection. Thus may they never fail in love, or lose the treasure of the holy faith, but rather, with all the hosts of

Angels and Saints, may they glorify Your boundless mercy for endless ages. Amen.

FOURTH DAY

TODAY BRING TO ME THOSE WHO DO NOT BELIEVE IN GOD AND THOSE WHO DO NOT YET KNOW ME. I was thinking also of them during My bitter Passion, and their future zeal comforted My heart. Immerse them in the ocean of My mercy".

Most Compassionate Jesus, You are the light of the whole world. Receive into the abode of Your Most Compassionate Heart the souls of those who as yet do not believe in you or do not know You. Let the rays of Your grace enlighten them that they, too, together with us, may extol Your wonderful mercy, and do not let them escape from the abode which is Your Most Compassionate Heart.

Eternal Father, turn Your merciful gaze upon the souls of those who do not believe in Your Son, and of those who as yet do not know You, but who are enclosed in the Most Compassionate Heart of Jesus. Draw them to the light of the Gospel. These souls do not know what great happiness it is to love You. Grant that they too, may extol the generosity of Your mercy for endless ages. Amen.

TODAY BRING TO ME THE SOULS OF THOSE WHO HAVE SEPARATED FROM MY CHURCH and immerse them in the ocean of My mercy. During My bitter Passion they tore at My Body and heart, that is, My church. As they return to unity with the Church, My wounds heal, and in this way they alleviate My Passion".

Most Merciful Jesus, Goodness Itself, You do not refuse light to those who seek it of You. Receive into the abode of Your Most Compassionate Heart the souls of those who have separated from your church. Draw them by Your light into the unity of the Church, and do not let them escape from the abode of Your Most Compassionate heart; but bring it about that they, too, come to glorify the generosity of Your mercy.

Eternal Father, turn Your merciful gaze upon the souls of those who are separated from your Son's church, especially those who have squandered Your blessings and misused Your graces by obstinately persisting in their errors. Do not look upon their errors, but upon the love of Your own Son and upon His bitter Passion, which He underwent for their sake, since they too, are enclosed in His Most Compassionate Heart. Bring it about that they also may glorify Your great mercy for endless ages. Amen.

TODAY BRING TO ME THE MEEK AND HUMBLE SOULS AND THE SOULS OF LITTLE CHILDREN and immerse them in My mercy. These souls most closely resemble My Heart. They strengthened Me during My bitter agony. I saw them as earthly Angels, who will keep vigil at My altars. I pour out upon them whole torrents of grace. Only the humble soul is capable of receiving My Grace. I favour humble souls with my confidence".

Most Merciful Jesus, You Yourself have said "Learn from Me for I am meek and humble of heart." Receive into the abode of Your Most Compassionate Heart all meek and humble souls and the souls of little children. These souls send all heaven into ecstasy, and they are the heavenly Father's favourites. They are a sweet-smelling bouquet before the throne of God; God himself takes delight in their fragrance. These souls have a permanent abode in Your Most Compassionate Heart, O Jesus, and they unceasingly sing out a hymn of love and mercy.

Eternal Father, turn Your merciful gaze upon meek and humble souls and upon the souls of little children, who are enfolded in the abode which is the Most Compassionate Heart of Jesus. These souls bear the closest resemblance to Your Son. Their fragrance rises from the earth and reaches Your very throne. Father of mercy and of all goodness, I beg You by the love You bear these souls and by the delight You take in them: bless the whole world, that all souls together may sing out the praises of Your mercy for endless ages. Amen.

SEVENTH DAY

TODAY BRING TO ME THE SOULS WHO ESPECIALLY VENERATE AND GLORIFY MY MERCY and immerse them in My mercy. These souls sorrowed most over My Passion and entered most deeply into My spirit. They are living images of My Compassionate Heart. These Souls will shine with a special brightness in the next life. Not one of them will go into the fire of hell. I shall particularly defend each one of them at the hour of death".

Most Merciful Jesus, whose Heart is love itself, receive into the abode of Your most compassionate Heart the souls of those who particularly extol and venerate the greatness of Your mercy. These souls are mighty with the very power of God Himself. In the midst of all afflictions and adversities they go forward confident of Your mercy. These souls are united to Jesus and carry all mankind on their shoulders. These souls will not be judged severely, but Your mercy will embrace them as they depart from this life.

Eternal Father, turn Your merciful gaze upon the souls who glorify and venerate Your greatest attribute, that of Your fathomless mercy, and who are enclosed in the Most Compassionate Heart of Jesus. These souls are a living Gospel; their hands are full of deeds of mercy and their spirits, overflowing with joy, sing a canticle of mercy to You, O Most High! I beg You O God: show them Your Mercy according to the hope and trust they have placed in You. Let there be accomplished in them the promise of Jesus, who said to them that during their life, but especially at the hour of death, the souls who will venerate this fathomless mercy of His, He Himself will defend as His glory. Amen.

EIGHTH DAY

TODAY BRING TO ME THE SOULS WHO ARE DETAINED IN PURGATORY and immerse them in the Abyss of My mercy. **Let the torrents of My Blood cool down their scorching flames. All these souls are greatly loved by Me. They are making retribution to My justice. It is in your power to bring them relief. Draw all the indulgences from the**

treasury of My Church and offer them on their behalf. Oh, if you only knew the torments they suffer, you would continually offer for them the alms of the spirit and pay off their debt for My justice".

Most Merciful Jesus, You Yourself have said that You desire mercy; so I bring into the abode of Your Most Compassionate Heart the souls in Purgatory, souls who are very dear to You, and yet who must make retribution to Your justice. May the streams of Blood and Water which gushed forth from Your Heart put out the flames of the purifying fire, that in that place, too, the power of Your mercy may be praised.

Eternal Father, turn Your merciful gaze upon the souls suffering in Purgatory, who are enfolded in the Most Compassionate Heart of Jesus. I beg you, by the sorrowful Passion of Jesus your Son, and by all the bitterness with which His Most Sacred Soul was flooded, manifest Your mercy to the souls who are under Your just scrutiny. Look upon them in no other way than through the Wounds of Jesus, Your dearly Beloved Son; for we firmly believe that there is no limit to Your goodness and compassion. Amen.

TODAY BRING TO ME SOULS WHO HAVE BECOME LUKE WARM and immerse them in the abyss of My mercy. These souls wound My Heart most painfully. My soul suffered the most dreadful loathing in the Garden of Olives because of luke warm souls. They were the reason I cried out: "Father, take this cup away from Me, if it be Your will". For them the last hope of salvation is to run to My mercy.

Most Compassionate Jesus, You are Compassion Itself. I bring lukewarm souls into the abode of Your Most Compassionate Heart. In this fire of Your pure love let these tepid souls, who, like corpses, filled You with such deep loathing, be once again set aflame. O Most Compassionate Jesus, exercise the omnipotence of Your mercy and draw them into the very ardour of Your love; and bestow upon them the gift of holy love, for nothing is beyond Your power.

Eternal Father, turn Your merciful gaze upon lukewarm souls who are nonetheless enfolded in the Most Compassionate Heart of Jesus. Father of Mercy, I beg You by the bitter Passion of Your Son and by His three-hour agony on the Cross, let them too, glorify the abyss of Your mercy. Amen.

DIVINE MERCY CONVERSION PRAYER

The prayer most pleasing to Me is the prayer for conversion. Know, My daughter, that this prayer is always heard and answered".
(Diary 1397).

Jesus said: "I desire that you know more profoundly the love that burns in My Heart for souls, and you will understand this when you meditate upon My Passion.

Call upon My Mercy on behalf of sinners; I desire their salvation. When you say this prayer, with a contrite heart and with faith on behalf of some sinner, I will give that soul the grace of conversion. This is the prayer: *(Diary 186)*

O Blood and Water, which gushed forth from the Heart of Jesus as a fount of mercy for us, I trust in You."

(Diary 187)

SAINT FAUSTINA'S
PRAYER FOR HEALING

Jesus, may Your pure and healthy blood circulate in my ailing organism, and may Your pure and healthy body transform my weak unhealthy body, and may a healthy and vigorous life flow within me, if it is truly Your holy will, Amen.

SAINT FAUSTINA'S
PRAYER FOR PRIESTS

O My Jesus,
I beg You on behalf of the whole Church:
grant it love and the light of Your Spirit,
give power to the words of priests
so that hardened hearts
might be brought to repentance
and return to You.
Lord, give us holy priests;
You yourself maintain them in holiness.
O Divine and Great High Priest
may the power of Your mercy
accompany them everywhere and protect them
from the devil's traps and snares which are
continually being set for the souls of priests.
May the power of Your mercy, O Lord,
shatter and bring to naught
all that might tarnish the sanctity of priests,
for You can do all things.

PRAYER TO BE MERCIFUL
Love one another as I have loved you (Jn: 15.12)

Help me Jesus, that what I ask of You (Mercy) I will give to others in word and deed.

Help me, O Lord, that my eyes may be merciful, so that I may never suspect or judge others, but always look for what is beautiful and good in other people. Help me, that my ears may be merciful, so that I may give heed to others needs, and not be indifferent to their pain.

Help me, O Lord, that my tongue may be merciful, so that I should never speak wrongly of others, but have a word of comfort and forgiveness for all.

Help me, O Lord, that my hands may be merciful and filled with good deeds so that I may do only good to others and always try to take upon myself the more difficult tasks.

Help me, O Lord, that my feet may be merciful, so that I may hurry to assist others, overcoming my own fatigue and weariness, contemplating Your love and mercy.

Help me, O Lord, to forgive and forget. This is Your greatest gift to me, and should be mine for Your sake, to all who offend me. *(Based on Diary 163)*

The love of God is the flower - Mercy the fruit.
Let the doubting soul read these considerations on Divine Mercy and become trusting:

Divine Mercy, gushing forth from the bosom of the Father,   **I trust in You**.

Divine Mercy, greatest attribute of God,
                                                    I trust in You.

Divine Mercy, incomprehensible mystery,
                                                    I trust in You.

Divine Mercy, fount gushing forth from the mystery of the Most Blessed Trinity,
                                                    I trust in You.

Divine Mercy, unfathomable by any intellect human or angelic,   **I trust in You.**

Divine Mercy, from which wells forth all life and happiness,   **I trust in You.**

Divine Mercy, better than the heavens,
                                                    I trust in You.

Divine Mercy, source of miracles and wonders,
                                                    I trust in You.

Divine Mercy, encompassing the whole universe,
                                                    I trust in You.

Divine Mercy, descending to earth in the Person of the Incarnate Word,   **I trust in You.**

Divine Mercy which flowed out from the open

wound of the Heart of Jesus,   **I trust in You.**

Divine Mercy enclosed in the Heart of Jesus for us and especially for sinners,   **I trust in You.**

Divine Mercy unfathomed in the institution of the Sacred Host,   **I trust in You.**

Divine Mercy, in the founding of the Holy Church,   **I trust in You.**

Divine Mercy, in the sacrament of Holy Baptism,   **I trust in You.**

Divine Mercy, in our justification through Jesus Christ,   **I trust in You.**

Divine Mercy, accompanying us through our whole life,   **I trust in You.**

Divine Mercy, embracing us especially at the hour of death,   **I trust in You.**

Divine Mercy, endowing us with immortal life,   **I trust in You**.

Divine Mercy, accompanying us every moment of our life,   **I trust in You.**

Divine Mercy, shielding us from the fire of hell,   **I trust in You.**

Divine Mercy, in the conversion of hardened sinners,   **I trust in You.**

Divine Mercy, astonishment for angels, incomprehensible to saints,   **I trust in You.**

Divine Mercy, unfathomed in all the mysteries of God, **I trust in You**.

Divine Mercy, lifting us out of every misery, **I trust in You.**

Divine Mercy, source of our happiness and joy, **I trust in You.**

Divine Mercy, in calling us forth from nothingness to existence, **I trust in You.**

Divine Mercy, embracing all the works of His hands, **I trust in You.**

Divine Mercy, crown of all God's handy work, **I trust in You.**

Divine Mercy, in which we are all immersed, **I trust in You.**

Divine Mercy, sweet relief for anguished hearts, **I trust in You.**

Divine Mercy, only hope of despairing souls, **I trust in You.**

Divine Mercy, repose of hearts, peace amidst fear, **I trust in You**.

Divine Mercy, delight and ecstasy of holy souls, **I trust in You.**

Divine Mercy, inspiring hope against all hope, **I trust in You.**

SAY THIS PRAYER WHEN IN DESPAIR

Eternal God in whom mercy is endless
and the treasury of compassion
inexhaustible,

Look kindly on us and
increase your mercy in us
so that in difficult moments
we might not despair nor become
despondent,
but with great confidence
submit ourselves to your holy will
which is love and mercy itself.

O incomprehensible and limitless
Mercy Divine, who can extol and
adore You worthily?

HELP US FULFIL YOUR HOLY WILL

Eternal Father, You show Your almighty power most of all in Your forgiveness and mercy, we thank You for the graces You granted Your servant, Saint Faustina. Grant that we may follow her example, and supported by her intercession, fulfil Your Holy Will in everything. Through Christ Our Lord, Amen.

A NOVENA TO OBTAIN GRACES THROUGH THE INTERCESSION OF SAINT FAUSTINA

Jesus, You gave your servant, Saint Faustina, the gift of deep reverence for Your unending mercy. I ask You if it be Your holy will, to grant me, through her prayers, the grace for which I fervently pray...(*mention your need*)

Because of my sins, I don't deserve Your Mercy, but I ask You to remember Saint Faustina's spirit of sacrifice and self-denial, and to be gracious to her faithful love of You by granting the petition which I make to You now, with childlike trust through her intercession. Amen.

SAINT JOSEPH AND DEVOTION
TO THE DIVINE MERCY

Saint Faustina wrote in her Diary: "Saint Joseph urged me to have a constant devotion to him. He himself told me to recite everyday three prayers, and the *'Remember...'* once. He looked at me with great kindness and gave me to know how much he is supporting this work (of mercy). He has promised me his special help and protection. I recite the requested prayers every day and feel his special protection." *(Diary 1203).*

The "three prayers" referred to are the *Our Father, the Hail Mary, and the Glory be to the Father...*

The "Remember" is the prayer to St. Joseph that her religious community recited daily:

PRAYER TO ST. JOSEPH

Remember, O most pure spouse of Mary, and my dearly beloved guardian, St. Joseph, that never was it known that anyone who invoked your care and requested your help was left without consolation.

Inspired with this confidence, I come to you, and with all the ardor of my spirit I commend myself to you. Do not reject my prayer, O Foster Father of the Saviour, but graciously receive and answer it. Amen.

PRAYER TO THE DIVINE MERCY

O Lord, behold here before You a soul who exists in this world in order to allow You to exercise Your admirable MERCY and manifest it before heaven and earth. Others may glorify You through their faithfulness and perseverance, thus making evident the power of Your grace. How sweet and generous You are to those who are faithful to You!

Nevertheless I will glorify You by acquainting others of Your goodness to sinners and by reminding them that Your MERCY is above all malice, that nothing can exhaust it, and that no relapse, no matter how shameful or criminal, should allow the sinner to despair of forgiveness.

I have offended You grievously, O beloved Redeemer, but it would be still worse if I were to offend You by thinking that You were lacking in goodness to forgive me. I would rather be deprived of everything else than the TRUST I have in Your MERCY.

Should I fall a hundred times, or should my crimes be a hundred times worse than they actually are, I would continue to trust in Your MERCY.

Prayer of Saint Claude De Columbiere
(Chosen by Saint Faustina as one of her patrons)

PRAYER FOR MERCY FOR THE DYING

O merciful Jesus, lover of souls, I beseech You, by the agony of Your Most Sacred Heart and by the sorrows of Your Immaculate Mother, wash clean in Your Blood the sinners of the whole world who are now in their final agony but especially those on their way to eternal damnation and who are to die this day. Heart of Jesus who suffered death's agony, I beg You have mercy on these poor souls.

PRAYER FOR MERCY FOR SOULS IN PURGATORY

Eternal Father, I offer You the most precious blood of Your Divine Son, Jesus, in union with the Masses said throughout the world today, for all the holy souls in Purgatory, for sinners everywhere, for sinners in the universal church, for those in my own home and within my own family. Amen

Prayer of Saint Gertrude
(Chosen by Saint Faustina as one of her patrons)

DIVINE MERCY PRAYER
FOR HOMELESS CHILDREN

Eternal Father ... reach out with Your tender love and mercy to those pitiful children who wander the streets at night.

With Your unfathomable love and mercy, bring them back to their families, or to a home You choose for them.

Jesus ... through Your Divine Mercy, enable us to help these poor children, with our deeds, and with our prayers.

Holy Spirit ... lead many to reach out in love to poor children in distress.

Mother Mary ... send out Your mother's love to those poor children who have never really known the love and tenderness of an earthly mother.

We unite this prayer with all the prayers of Divine Mercy offered to the Eternal Father this day for the lonely, distressed, and homeless children and people of the world.

Through **Jesus Christ , Our Lord.** Amen.

Prayer of Divine Mercy Apostolate, Dublin.

PRAYER FOR THE RELEASE OF A LOVED ONE FROM ALCOHOL OR DRUG ADDICTION THROUGH THE DIVINE MERCY AND BLOOD OF JESUS

Lord Jesus, I put myself into Your hands this day. I ask You with all my heart, to cure the terrible addiction to alcohol (drugs) in...*(name the person)*.

Create in them an intolerance for alcohol (drugs) that will prevent them from ever offending those who love them again.

And grant their loved ones the grace to forgive them for all the hurt they have caused.

Through the Divine Mercy and blood of Jesus, I also pray that they will be healed of all withdrawal symptoms of this terrible affliction.

I sincerely ask this, in the name of Jesus. Amen.

Prayer of Divine Mercy Apostolate Dublin.

DIVINE MERCY FOR THE PHYSICALLY AND SEXUALLY ABUSED

Divine Mercy I beg of you to protect all those helpless children who are physically and sexually abused, especially by those whose duty it is to guide and protect them on earth.

Send down Your enveloping cloak of Mercy and wrap it around these poor children and enfold them in Your love and protection.

Send forth Your rays of blood and water to cleanse and renew the souls of those who perpetrate these vile acts of Satan.

Let there be a way to get Your powerful image of Divine Mercy into the homes of these sad families, from where graces will flow as You promise, and they shall be renewed.

O blood and water which gushed forth from The Heart of Jesus as a fount of Mercy for us, I trust in You.

Prayer of Divine Mercy Apostolate Dublin.

DIVINE MERCY, DIRECT ME

Eternal God, Goodness itself, whose mercy is incomprehensible to every intellect, whether human or angelic, help me, your feeble child, to do Your holy will as You make it known to me. I desire nothing but to fulfil God's desires. Lord, here is my soul and my body, my mind and my will, my heart and all my love. Direct me according to Your eternal plan. *(Diary 492)*

PRAYER FOR THE TROUBLED AND DESPONDENT

O God, we thank and praise You for the
gift of life - Your gift to each one of us,
given a day at a time.
Let us never be over anxious about the future,
but leave it in the hands of God.
Each day arranged by Him is His gift,
His act of love for each of us.
Lord, enlighten and comfort those who,
through pain, fear, despair or any evil influence, may be tempted to injure or destroy the precious gift of life entrusted to them.

Fr. Donatus McNamara O.F.M.Cap
(Divine Mercy Apostolate, Dublin)

PRAYER FOR A LONELY SOUL

Jesus, Friend of a lonely heart,
You are my haven, You are my peace.
You are my salvation,
You are my serenity in moments of struggle
and amidst an ocean of doubts.
You are the bright ray that lights up the path
of my life. You are everything to a lonely soul.
You understand the soul even though it
remains silent. You know our weaknesses and
You comfort and heal, sparing us sufferings.
(Diary 247)

DIVINE MERCY FOR THE UNBORN

For all helpless little children who die in the
womb of their mother, I pray that all of these
little souls will be given eternal life by Our Lord,
Jesus Christ, through his Divine Mercy and I beg
Jesus that I be allowed to spiritually baptise a
little soul born dead and I do so by saying:
I baptise you *(give name, preferably a Saint's name)*
in the name of the Father and of the Son and of
the Holy Spirit... I have called you by your name,
you are Mine! *(Is.43:1)*

Prayer of Divine Mercy Apostolate, Dublin

PRAYER OF CONSECRATION TO THE DIVINE MERCY

Jesus, the Divine Mercy, I consecrate my entire
life, from this day on, to You without reserve.
Into Your hands I abandon my past,
my present, and my future,
from this day forward,
make me a true follower of Your teaching
let Your Divine Mercy Image protect my home
and my family from all the powers of evil
in this world today.
May all who venerate it never perish,
may it be their joy in life, their hope in death,
and their glory in eternity. Amen.

PRAYER FOR GRANDPARENTS

Dear Saint Anne and Joachim, you who were
Grandparents to Baby Jesus, pray for us.
You who knew the anguish of parenthood,
Pray for us. Pray that we will accept the plan
of the almighty, and that we will place all our
trust in the Lord, and accept the role He
demands of us in life. Pray that we may be
blessed by our grandchildren and know that
each and every one is a special gift, chosen
and given by the Lord to us. Amen

PRAYER OF CONSECRATION TO MARY THE MOTHER OF MERCY

O Mary, my Mother and my Lady,
I offer you my soul, my body, my life,
and my death, and all that will come after it.

I place everything in your hands.
O, my Mother, cover my soul
with your Virginal mantle, and grant me
the grace of purity of heart, soul and body.

Defend me with your power against
all enemies, but especially against those
who hide their malice behind a mask of virtue.

O, Mary You are my joy, because through you,
God descended to earth and into my heart.

DIVINE MERCY PRAYER FOR VOCATIONS

Lord Jesus, transform the hearts and lives of those You are calling to serve as priests, brothers and sisters in your Church.

Make them living reflections of Your Heart and channels of Your Mercy to others.

Open their eyes to see Your presence in souls around them; open their ears to the appeals of others; inspire them with Your message of forgiveness and comfort; strengthen them for the service of those in need as You prepare them to reflect Your Mercy.

Lord Jesus, call many generous souls to Your service, and transform them into ministers of Your Mercy, for You can do all things. Amen.

DIVINE MERCY PRAYER FOR ALL MANKIND, ESPECIALLY FOR SINNERS

Most Merciful Jesus, whose very nature it is to have compassion and forgive us,

do not look upon our sins, but on the trust we place in Your infinite goodness.

We beg You, turn Your merciful gaze on all mankind and especially upon poor sinners,

enfold them in Your Most Compassionate Heart, that we may praise the infinite power of Your Mercy for ever.

Amen .

DIVINE MERCY WAY OF THE CROSS

Begin each station with: Eternal Father, I offer You the Body and Blood, Soul and Divinity of Your dearly beloved Son, Our Lord Jesus Christ, in atonement for my sins and those of the whole world.

First Station
Jesus condemned to death

My Jesus so meek and uncomplaining, teach me resignation in trials. Have mercy on me and on the whole world.

Second Station
Jesus carries His Cross

My Jesus, this Cross should be mine, not Yours: my sins crucified You. Have mercy on me and on the whole world.

Third Station
Our Lord falls the First Time

My Jesus, by this first fall, never let me fall into mortal sin. Have mercy on me and on the whole world.

✛   ✛   ✛   ✛   ✛   ✛

Station I.
Jesus condemned to death

Station II.
Jesus carries His cross

Station III.
Our Lord Falls for the First Time

Station IV.
Jesus Meets His Mother

Station V.
Simon of Cyrenean helps Jesus carry His Cross

Station VI.
Veronica wipes the Face of Jesus

Station VII.
Our Lord Falls for the Second Time

Station VIII.
Jesus consoles the women of Jerusalem

Station IX.
Our Lord Falls for the Third Time

Jesus I Trust in You

The Way of the Cross

Station X.
Jesus Stripped of His Garments

Station XI.
Jesus nailed to the Cross

Station XII.
Jesus dies on the Cross

Station XIII.
Jesus taken down from the Cross

Station XIV.
Jesus laid in the Sepulchre

Fourth Station
Jesus meets His Mother

My Jesus, may no human tie, however dear, keep me from following the road of the Cross. Have mercy on me and on the whole world.

Fifth Station
Simon of Cyrene helps Jesus carry His Cross.

Simon unwillingly assisted You; may I, with patience, suffer all for You. Have mercy on me and on the whole world.

Sixth Station
Veronica wipes the Face of Jesus

My Jesus You did imprint Your Sacred features upon Veronica's veil; stamp them indelibly upon my heart. Have mercy on me and on the whole world.

Seventh Station
The Second Fall of Jesus

By Your second fall, preserve me, dear Lord, from relapse into sin. Have mercy on me and on the whole world.

Eight Station
Jesus consoles the women of Jerusalem

My greatest consolation would be to hear You say: "Many sins are forgiven You, because You have loved so much." Have mercy on me and on the whole world.

Ninth Station
Third Fall of Jesus

O Jesus when weary upon life's long journey, be my strength and my perseverance. Have mercy on me and on the whole world.

Tenth Station
Jesus stripped of His Garments

My soul has been robbed of its robe of innocence; clothe me, dear Jesus, with the garb of penance and contrition. Have mercy on me and on the whole world.

Eleventh Station
Jesus nailed to the Cross

You forgave Your enemies; my God, teach me to forgive mine. Have mercy on me and on the whole world.

Twelfth Station
Jesus dies on the Cross

You are dying, My Jesus, but Your Sacred Heart still throbs with love for Your sinful children. Have mercy on me and on the whole world.

Thirteenth Station
Jesus taken down from the Cross

Receive me into Your arms, O sorrowful Mother and obtain for me perfect contrition for my sins. Ask Your Son to have mercy on me and on the whole world.

Fourteenth Station
Jesus laid in the Sepulchre

When I receive You into my heart in Holy Communion, O Jesus, make it a fit and abiding place for Your Adorable Body. Have mercy on me and on the whole world.

M ary, My Mother, I place everything in your hands *(Diary 79)*...You are joy, because through you God descended to earth and into my heart," *(Diary 40)*.

Hail Holy Queen, Mother of mercy..." For centuries people have invoked Mary under this title, and now in modern times, Pope John Paul II presented it to us again to emphasise the unique role Mary plays in God's eternal plan of mercy. In his encyclical letter, *Rich in Mercy*, he devotes an entire section to Mary, the "Mother of Mercy". She is the one, he explains, who has the deepest understanding of God's mercy, the one who, more than anyone else, deserved and received mercy. Called in a special way to share her Son's mission to reveal His Love, she continues to proclaim His mercy "from generation to generation."

For Saint Faustina, Mary was a constant source of God's mercy, as mother, guardian, teacher and intercessor. From Mary she received a special gift of purity, strength in suffering, and countless lessons on the spiritual life. "Mary is my instructress," she writes, "who is ever teaching me how to live for God *(Diary 620)*...The more I imitate the Mother of God, the more deeply I get to know God *(Diary 843)*...before every Holy Communion, I earnestly ask the Mother of God to help me prepare my soul for the coming of her Son *(Diary 1114)*... She has taught me how to love God interiorly and also how to carry out His will in all things." *(Diary 40)*

TO THE MOTHER OF DIVINE MERCY

O Mary, my Mother and my Lady, I offer You my soul, my body, my life and my death, and all that will come after it. I place everything in Your hands. O my Mother, cover my soul with your Virginal mantle and grant me the grace of purity of heart, soul and body. Defend me with your power against all enemies, and especially against those who hide their malice behind the mask of virtue *(Diary 75)*... Fortify my soul that pain may not break it. Mother of grace, teach me to live by God's power *(Diary 315)*.

O Mary, a terrible sword has pierced your holy soul. Except for God, no one knows of your suffering. Your soul does not break; it is brave, because it is with Jesus, Sweet Mother, unite my soul to Jesus, because it is only then that I will be able to endure all trials and tribulations, and only in union with Jesus will my little sacrifices be pleasing to God.

Sweetest Mother, continue to teach me about the interior life. May the sword of suffering never break me. O pure Virgin, pour courage into my heart and guard it *(Diary 215)*.

ENTRANCE ANTIPHON

The favours of the Lord, I will sing forever. Through all generations my mouth shall proclaim Your faithfulness.

OPENING PRAYER

All powerful and ever-living God, You chose Saint Faustina to proclaim the boundless richness of Your Mercy. Grant that we may learn from her example to trust in Your Mercy completely, and to perform acts of Christian love with perseverance. We ask this through Our Lord Jesus Christ, Your Son, who lives and reigns with You and the Holy Spirit, one God, for ever and ever.

Appropriate Readings

FIRST READING

From the book of the prophet Hosea
2:16-17,21-22

I will lead her into the desert and speak to her heart. From there I will give her the vineyards she had, and the valley of Achor as a door of hope. She shall respond there as in the days of her youth, when she came up from the land of Egypt.

I will espouse you to Me forever. I will espouse in right and in justice, in love and in mercy; I will espouse you in fidelity, and you shall know the Lord.

This is the Word of the Lord.

RESPONSORIAL PSALM
Ps 103/102: 1-2, 3-4, 8-9, 11-12

R. The Lord is Gracious, full of mercy

Bless the Lord, O my soul, and all my being,
bless His Holy name.
Bless the Lord, O my soul, and forget not
all His benefits.
Response.

He pardons all your iniquities,
He heals all your ills.
He redeems your life from destruction,
He crowns you with kindness and compassion.
Response.

Merciful and gracious is the Lord,
slow to anger and abounding in kindness.
He will not always chide,
nor does He keep His wrath forever.
Response.

For as the heavens are high above the earth, so surpassing is His kindness toward those who fear Him.

As far as the east is from the west,
so far has He put our transgressions from us.
Response.

From the letter of Paul to the Ephesians
3 : 8-12,14-19

To me, the very least of all the holy ones, this grace was given, to preach to the Gentiles the inscrutable riches of Christ, and to bring to light for all, what is the plan of the mystery hidden from ages past in God, Who created all things, so that the manifold wisdom of God might now be made known through the church, to the principalities and authorities in the heavens. This was according to the eternal purpose, that He accomplished in Christ Jesus Our Lord, in whom we have boldness of speech, and confidence of access, through faith in Him.

For this reason I kneel before the Father, from Whom every family in heaven and on earth is named, that He may grant you in accord with the riches of His glory, to be strengthened with power, through His Spirit in the inner self, and that Christ may dwell in your hearts, through faith; that you, rooted and grounded in love, may have strength to comprehend, with all the holy ones, what is the breadth, and length and height, and depth, and to know the love of Christ, that surpasses knowledge, so that you be filled with all the fullness of God.

This is the Word of the Lord.

GOSPEL
1Jn 4:10

Alleluia, Alleluia: In this is love: not that we have loved God, but that He loved us and sent His Son as expiation for our sins. Alleluia.

From the Holy Gospel according to John.
Jn 19:31-37

Now since it was preparation day, in order that the bodies might not remain on the cross on the sabbath, for the sabbath day of that week was a solemn one, the Jews asked Pilate that their legs be broken and they be taken down. So the soldiers came and broke the legs of the first and then of the other one who was crucified with Jesus. But when they came to Jesus and saw that He was already dead, they did not break His legs, but one soldier thrust his lance into His side, and immediately blood and water flowed out. An eyewitness has testified, and his testimony is true; he knows that he is speaking the truth, so that you also may come to believe. For this happened so that the scripture passage might be fulfilled: "Not a bone in His body will be broken." And again another passage says: "They will look upon Him, Whom they have pierced."

This is the Gospel of the Lord.

PRAYER OVER THE GIFTS

God our Father, accept these gifts we offer You with joy. Make us, together with Christ, an expiatory sacrifice for our sins and those of the whole world.

COMMUNION ANTIPHON

Give thanks to the Lord for He is good for His mercy endures forever. (Ps. 118/117)

PRAYER AFTER COMMUNION

God rich in Mercy, may the Blessed Sacrament renew our Souls and bodies so that by Saint Faustina's example we may be able to bring the hope of Your mercy to the whole world. Amen.

PRAYERS EVERY CATHOLIC SHOULD KNOW

The Holy Rosary is composed of twenty decades, each decade consisting of the Our Father, the Hail Mary, and the Glory be to the Father; and each being recited in honour of some mystery in the life of Our Lord and of His Blessed Mother.

During each decade, we should call to mind the mystery which it is intended to honour, and pray that we may learn to practise the virtue specially taught us by that mystery.

A plenary indulgence may be gained, under the usual conditions for the recitation of the Rosary (five decades are sufficient), in a church or public oratory or in the family. If the Rosary is said privately a partial indulgence may be gained.

THE FIVE JOYFUL MYSTERIES
1. The Annunciation. *(Luke 1.26-38)*
2. The Visitation. *(Luke 1.39-50)*
3. The Birth of Our Lord. *(Luke 1.14)*
4. The Presentation in the Temple. *(Luke 2.22-35)*
5. The Finding of Jesus in the Temple *(Luke 2.42-52)*

THE FIVE SORROWFUL MYSTERIES
1. The Agony in the Garden. *(Matt.26.36-46)*
2. The Scourging at the Pillar. *(Matt.27.17-26)*
3. The Crowning with Thorns. *(Matt.27.27-30)*

4 . The Carrying of the Cross. *(Matt.27. 31-32)*
5. The Crucifixion *(John 19.17-42)*

THE FIVE GLORIOUS MYSTERIES
1. The Resurrection. *(Matt.28.1-8)*
2. Ascension of Christ into Heaven. *(Acts 1.6-11)*
3. The Descent of the Holy Spirit *(Acts 2.1-13)*
4. The Assumption. *(Redemptoris Mater)*
5. Coronation of the Virgin Mary *(Rev. 12.1-2)*

THE FIVE LUMINOUS MYSTERIES
1. The Baptism of Jesus' in the Jordan *(Matt. 3. 13)*
2. The Wedding at Cana *(Jn. 2.1-12)*
3. Jesus' Proclaims the Kingdom
    (Matt. 1.15, 2. 3-13)
4. Jesus' Transfiguration *(Luke. 9. 34)*
5. Institution of the Eucharist *(Jn. 6. 22- 65)*

Then is said:
Hail, Holy Queen, Mother of Mercy; hail our life, our sweetness and our hope. To you do we cry, poor banished children of Eve; to you do we send up our sighs, mourning and weeping in this valley of tears. Turn then, most gracious advocate, your eyes of mercy towards us; and after this our exile, show unto us the blessed fruit of your womb, Jesus.
O Clement, O loving, O Sweet Virgin Mary.
V. Pray for us O Holy Mother of God.
R. That we may be made worthy of the promises of Christ.

Let us pray.

O God, whose only begotten Son, by His life, death and resurrection, has purchased for us the rewards of eternal life; grant, we beseech You, that while meditating on these mysteries of the most holy Rosary of the Blessed Virgin Mary, we may imitate what they contain, and obtain what they promise, through the same Christ Our Lord. Amen.

THE FIFTEEN PROMISES OF MARY TO CHRISTIANS WHO RECITE THE ROSARY

1. Whoever shall faithfully serve me by the recitation of the Rosary, shall receive signal (extraordinary) graces.

2. I promise my special protection and the greatest graces to all those who shall recite the Rosary.

3. The Rosary shall be a powerful armour against hell, it will destroy vice, decrease sin, and defeat heresies.

4. It will cause virtue and good works to flourish: it will obtain for souls the abundant mercy of God; it will withdraw the hearts of people from the love of the world and its vanities, and will lift them to the desire of eternal things. Oh, that souls would sanctify themselves by these means!

5. The soul which recommends itself to me by the   recitation of the Rosary, shall not perish.

6. Whoever shall recite the Rosary devoutly, applying themselves to the consideration of its   sacred mysteries shall never be conquered by misfortune. God will not chastise them in His justice, they shall not perish by an unprovided death; if they be just they shall remain in the grace of God, and become worthy of eternal life.

7. Whoever shall have a true devotion for the Rosary shall not die without the sacraments of the Church.

8. Those who are faithful to recite the Rosary shall have during their life and at their death the light of God and the plenitude of His graces; at the moment of death they shall participate in the merits of the saints in paradise.

9. I shall deliver from purgatory those who have been devoted to the Rosary.

10. The faithful children of the Rosary shall merit a high degree of glory in heaven.

11. You shall obtain all you ask of me by the recitation of the Rosary.

12. All those who propagate the holy Rosary shall be aided by me in their necessities.

13. I have obtained from my Divine Son that all the advocates of the Rosary shall have for intercessors the entire celestial court during their life and at the hour of death.

14. All those who recite the Rosary are my sons and daughters, and children of my only son Jesus Christ.

15. Devotion to my Rosary is a great sign of predestination.

(Given to St. Dominic and Blessed Alan. Imprimatur + Patrick J. Hays, D.D. Archbishop of New York.)

THE APOSTLES CREED

I believe in God, the Father Almighty, Creator of Heaven and Earth, and in Jesus Christ, His only Son, our Lord, Who was conceived by the Holy Spirit, born of the Virgin Mary, suffered under Pontius Pilate, was crucified, died, and was buried. He descended into Hell. The third day he rose again from the dead; He ascended into Heaven, and is seated at the right hand of God the Father Almighty. From thence He shall come to judge the living and the dead. I believe in the Holy Spirit, the holy Catholic Church, the communion of saints, the forgiveness of sins, the resurrection of the body, and life everlasting. Amen.

THE CONFITEOR

I confess to almighty God and to you, my brothers and sisters, that I have greatly sinned in my thoughts and in my words, in what I have done and in what I have failed to do, through my fault, through my fault, through my most grievous fault; therefore I ask blessed Mary ever-Virgin, all the Angels and Saints, and you, my brothers and sisters, to pray for me to the Lord our God.

SHORT ACT OF CONTRITION

O my God, because You are so good, I am very sorry that I have sinned against You and by the help of Your grace, I will not sin again.

THE ANGELUS

May be said at morning, noon or night, to put us in mind that God the Son became man for our salvation.

V. The angel of the Lord declared unto Mary:
R. And she conceived of the Holy Spirit.
Hail Mary etc.

V. Behold the handmaid of the Lord:
R. Be it done unto me according to Your word.
Hail Mary etc.

V. And the Word was made Flesh:
R. And dwelt among us. Hail Mary etc.

V. Pray for us, O holy Mother of God.
R. That we may be made worthy of the promises of Christ.

Let us pray
Pour forth, we beseech You, O Lord, Your grace into our hearts, that, we, to whom the incarnation of Christ, Your Son, was made known by the message of an angel, may, by His passion and cross, be brought to the glory of His resurrection, through the same Christ, Our Lord.
R. Amen.

May the divine assistance remain always with us and may the souls of the faithful departed, through the mercy of God, rest in peace.
R. Amen

REGINA CAELI

The Regina Caeli is a prayer that replaces the Angelus during the Easter Season from Holy Saturday to the Saturday after Pentecost.

The prayer is included in the Enchiridion (book) of Indulgences.

Queen of heaven, rejoice, alleluia:
For He whom you merited to bear, alleluia,
Has risen, as he said, alleluia.
Pray for us to God, alleluia.

V. Rejoice and be glad, O Virgin Mary, alleluia.

R. Because the Lord is truly risen, alleluia.

Let Us Pray.

O God, Who by the Resurrection of Your Son, our Lord Jesus Christ, granted joy to the whole world, grant, we beg You, that through the intercession of the Virgin Mary, His Mother, we may lay hold of the joys of eternal life. Through the same Christ our Lord.

R. Amen.

THE MEMORARE

Remember, O most gracious Virgin Mary, that never was it known, that anyone who fled to your protection, implored your help or sought your intercession, was left unaided. Inspired with this confidence I fly to You, O Virgin of Virgins, my Mother. To you I come, before you I stand, sinful and sorrowful. O Mother of the word incarnate, despise not my petition, but in Your mercy, hear and answer me. Amen.

PRAYER TO SAINT MICHAEL

Saint Michael the Archangel, defend us in our hour of need; be our safeguard against the wickedness and snares of the devil; may God restrain him, we humbly pray; and do thou, O Prince of the Heavenly Host, by the Power of God, thrust Satan into hell and with him all evil spirits, who wander through the world for the ruin of souls. Amen.

BASIC
CHRISTIAN
DOCTRINE

THE TEN COMMANDMENTS OF GOD

1. I am the Lord your God and you shall not have strange Gods before Me.
2. You shall not take the name of the Lord your God in vain.
3. Remember that you keep holy the Sabbath day (Sunday).
4. Honour your father and your mother.
5. You shall not kill.
6. You shall not commit adultery.
7. You shall not steal.
8. You shall not bear false witness against your neighbour.
9. You shall not covet (desire) your neighbour's wife.
10. You shall not covet (desire) your neighbour's goods.

PRECEPTS OF THE CHURCH

1. To keep the Sundays and Holy days of Obligation holy, by hearing Mass and resting from servile works.
2. To keep the days of Fasting and Abstinence appointed by the Church.
3. To go to Confession at least once a year.
4. To receive the Blessed Sacrament at least once a year, at Easter or thereabouts.

5. To contribute to the support of your priests.
6. Not to marry within certain degrees of kindred without dispensation.

THE SEVEN SACRAMENTS

1. **Baptism**: by which we are made Christians; children of God, members of His holy Church and heirs to the kingdom of Heaven.

2. **Confirmation:** by which we receive the Holy Spirit, to make us strong Christians and imbue us with the Spirit of Mercy

3. **The Holy Eucharist:** which is really and truly and substantially the Body and Blood, the Soul and Divinity of Jesus Christ under the appearances of bread and wine. The Holy Eucharist is not only a Sacrament, in which we receive our Divine Lord for the food and nourishment of our souls, and in which He is really present to be adored upon the altar; it is also a sacrifice, the Sacrifice of the Holy Mass, in which, at the time of consecration, the bread and wine are changed into the Body and Blood of Jesus Christ, and in which He is offered up for us to His Eternal Father.

4. **Penance:** by which the sins committed after Baptism are forgiven, and one of the greatest sources of God's mercy.

5. **Anointing of the Sick:** which, a blessing for healing in a dangerous illness, or prayers to prepare a dying person's soul for death, by providing absolution for sins by atonement, sacramental grace and prayers for the relief of suffering through anointing, and final administration of the Eucharist. This final Eucharist is known as "viaticum", which is Latin for provision for the journey.

6. **Holy Orders**: by which Bishops, Priests and other Ministers of the Church receive power and grace to perform their sacred duties.

7. **Matrimony:** which is the Sacrament of Christian Marriage.

THE SEVEN DEATHLY SINS

Pride
Covetousness
Lust
Anger
Gluttony
Envy
Sloth

THE VIRTUES

The Three Theological Virtues:
Faith, Hope and Charity.

The Four Cardinal Virtues:
Prudence, Justice, Fortitude, Temperance,

The Seven Gifts of the Holy Spirit:
Wisdom, Understanding, Counsel, Piety,
Fortitude, Knowledge, Fear of the Lord.

The Twelve Fruits of the Holy Spirit:
Charity, Joy, Peace, Patience, Kindness,
Goodness, Forbearance, Mildness, Faith,
Modesty, Self restraint, Chastity.

The Seven Corporal Works of Mercy:
To feed the hungry;
to give drink to the thirsty;
to clothe the naked; to help the homeless;
to visit the sick; to visit the imprisoned;
to bury the dead.

The Seven Spiritual Works of Mercy:
Admonish sinners; instruct the uninformed;
counsel the doubtful; comfort the sorrowful;
be patient with those in error; forgive offenses;
pray for the living and the dead.

IMPORTANT DATES IN CHURCH CALENDAR

Advent: Begins on the Sunday nearest the 30th November, it is in preparation for Christmas, or the coming of Our Lord. Advent has four Sundays.

Christmas: Which celebrates the Birth of Our Lord, begins at the Christmas Vigil on the eve of Christmas and ends on the 6th January, the celebration of the Baptism of Our Lord.

Lent: This is a time in preparation for Easter, and begins on Ash Wednesday and ends with the Easter Vigil. Passion Sunday or Palm Sunday: This is the sixth Sunday of Lent and is the beginning of Holy Week.

Easter Vigil: This is on Easter Saturday night when the Church awaits the Resurrection of Christ.

Easter: This is the most important time in the Church year, when we remember the Passion, Death and Resurrection of Jesus Christ. It is known as the Easter Triduum. It begins with the evening Mass on Holy Thursday, and finishes with the evening prayers on Easter Sunday.

The Ascension: is usually celebrated on the fortieth day after Easter.

Pentecost: Celebrated fifty days after Easter to commemorate the descent of the Holy Spirit on the Apostles. It is also considered the birth of the Church.

Trinity Sunday: This is the Sunday after Pentecost, and celebrates the mystery of the Father, the Son and the Holy Spirit.

Corpus Christi: is the Thursday after Trinity Sunday, and celebrates the Body and Blood of Christ.

Fast and Abstinence: Ash Wednesday and Good Friday are the only two official fast days of the Church, although today the Church encourages us to fast more often, especially on Fridays, the day of Our Lord's Passion. This is the day when self-denial should be practiced. The form of self-denial, to be offered in union with Our Lord's suffering on the Cross, is left to the free choice of each individual. The age at which abstinence becomes binding is fourteen. The obligation of fasting is restricted to those who have completed their eighteenth year until they have begun their sixtieth. Since November

21st, 1964, the following rules apply at whatever time of day Holy Communion is received:

1 Water may be taken at any time.
2 Solid food and drinks may be taken up to one hour before Holy Communion.
3 The sick (not necessarily bed-ridden) may also take genuine medicines, solid or liquid as well as non-alcoholic drinks at any time before Communion. The fast from solid food and drink is about a quarter of an hour for the sick and aged and those attending them.

CONFESSION
Is the greatest way to experience God's mercy.

Before confession examine your conscience by going through the ten commandments. In the confessional make the sign of the cross and say, In the name of the Father and of the Son and of the Holy Spirit, Amen. Then say, "Bless me Father for I have sinned." (It is helpful if you mention the length of time since your last confession.) If you have been away a long time you can tell the priest you wish to make a general confession and he will ask questions which you just answer, sometimes it is easier this way.

Do not fear going to confession:

Most people today have difficulties with going to confession. Priests today are a lot more understanding and sympathetic to those fears, so do not hesitate to make them known to the Priest and he will help you. He is there to help and guide you, if asked.

Jesus said to Saint Faustina:

When you go to confession, know this, that I am waiting for you in the confessional. I am only hidden by the priest, but I myself act in the soul. Here the misery of the soul meets the God of Mercy. From this fount of Mercy souls draw graces solely with the vessel of trust. If their trust is great there is no limit to My generosity," *(Diary 1602)*

After telling your sins, say "for these and all the sins of my life, I am heartily sorry". The priest may talk to you for a short time and then give you penance and invite you to say a good act of contrition whilst he is giving absolution.

The Act of Contrition

O My God, I am heartily sorry for having offended You and I detest my sins because I fear the loss of heaven and the pain of Hell, but most of all because they offend You my

God, who are so good and deserving of all my love, and I firmly resolve with the help of your grace never more to offend you, and to amend my life. Amen.

The priest will finally say: *Go in the peace and love of Christ.* Go out of the confessional and say your penance in the Church.

COMMUNION

In His revelations to Saint Faustina Our Lord makes it very clear what He is offering to us in Holy Communion and how much it hurts Him when we treat His presence in the eucharist with indifference.

Jesus said to Saint Faustina:
My great delight is to unite Myself with souls... When I come to a human heart in Holy Communion, My hands are full of all kinds of graces which I want to give to that soul.

How painful it is to Me that souls so seldom unite themselves to Me in Holy Communion. *(Diary 1447)*

JESUS TO RELIGIOUS

It pains Me very much when religious souls receive the Sacrament of Love merely out of habit, as if they do not understand what this food is. I find neither faith nor love in their hearts. I go to such souls with great reluctance. It would be better if they did not receive... *(Diary 1288)*

FEAST DAYS

Jan. 1.	Mary, the Mother of God
Jan. 6.	Epiphany
Jan. 25.	Conversion of St. Paul
Jan. 28.	St.Thomas Aquinas
Feb. 2.	Presentation of Jesus
Feb. 6.	St. Pope Paul VI
Feb. 15	Blessed Michael Sopocko
Feb. 22.	St. Peter, first Pope
Mar. 8.	St. John of God
Mar. 17.	St. Patrick
Mar. 19.	St. Joseph, the husband of Mary
Mar. 25.	Annunciation by the Angel Gabriel to Mary
Apr. 25.	St. Mark the Evangelist
May 1.	St. Joseph the Worker
May 3.	St. Philip and St. James, Apostles
May 13	Our Lady of Fatima
May 14.	St. Matthias, Apostle
May 31.	Visitation by Mary to Elizabeth

June 11.	St. Barnabas, Apostle
June 13.	St. Anthony of Padua
June 24.	Birth of St. John the Baptist
June 29.	St. Peter and St. Paul, Apostles
July 3.	St. Thomas, Apostle
July 16.	Our Lady of Mount Carmel
July 22.	St. Mary Magdalene
July 25.	St. James, Apostle
July 31.	St. Ignatius Loyola
Aug. 6.	The Transfiguration
Aug. 8.	St. Dominic
Aug. 11.	St. Clare
Aug. 15.	Assumption of Mary to Heaven
Aug. 22.	Queenship of Mary
Aug. 24.	St. Bartholomew, Apostle
Aug. 29.	Beheading of St. John the Baptist
Sept. 5.	Mother Teresa Calcutta
Sept. 8.	Birthday of Mary
Sept. 14.	Triumph of the Cross
Sept. 15.	Our Lady of Sorrows
Sept. 21.	St. Matthew, Apostle
Sept. 27.	St. Vincent De Paul
Sept. 29.	Archangels Michael, Gabriel and Raphael
Oct. 1.	St. Theresa of the Child Jesus
Oct. 2.	Guardian Angels

Oct.4.	St. Francis of Assisi
Oct. 5.	Saint Faustina
Oct. 7.	Our Lady of the Rosary
Oct. 9	St. John Henry Newman
Oct. 11	St. Pope John XXIII
Oct. 18.	St. Luke, Evangelist
Oct. 22.	St. Pope John Paul II
Oct. 28.	St. Simon and St. Jude, Apostles
Nov. 1.	All Saints
Nov. 2.	All Souls
Nov. 3.	St. Martin De Porres
Nov. 21.	Presentation of Mary
Nov. 30.	St. Andrew, Apostle
Dec. 3.	Francis Xavier
Dec. 8.	Immaculate Conception
Dec. 21.	Peter Canisius
Dec. 25.	Christmas, the birth of Jesus
Dec. 26.	St. Stephen
Dec. 27.	John, Apostle and Evangelist
Dec. 28.	Holy Innocents

*Sunday After Easter Sunday:
(Feast of Divine Mercy)

Ugo Festa was born in Vicenza, Italy, in 1951. He was struck down at an early age with multiple sclerosis. Gradually his health deteriorated. This led to many other problems in his young life. By the age of 39 he was suffering from multiple sclerosis, muscular dystrophy and epilepsy. Early in 1990 his spine was becoming distorted and he was having seizures daily. He had been continually attending doctors since he first contracted these conditions, at the time they could do nothing for him. He decided there was nothing left to try but prayer.

On the 28th April 1990 Ugo went with a pilgrimage to Rome. In his unfortunate situation he was introduced to Mother Teresa who was in Rome with a group of religious whom he also became acquainted with. Ugo was invited along with this group to a retreat at the shrine of Divine Mercy in Trent, but he refused. On leaving, one of the group, a nun, gave him five copies of the Divine Image Picture and a Divine Mercy medal. The following day the 29th April 1990 Ugo wore the medal and carried in his arms the images to be blessed at the papal audience at the Vatican. At the bottom of the steps to St. Peter's the Holy Father passed by. Ugo asked him to bless his Divine Mercy pictures. After blessing the pictures

"How Could You have a Crisis with Divine Mercy in Your Arms"

118

the Pope asked him how he felt. Ugo told him he felt very despondent and was at a crisis in his life. The Holy Father said **"How could you have a crisis with Jesus the Divine Mercy in your arms?** Entrust yourself to him and pray to my Sr. Faustina to intercede for you."* (This great moment is recorded in one of the photographs on the previous page.)* With this advice Ugo changed his mind and decided that he would go to the Divine Mercy Shrine in Trent. At the side altar in the Villa O'Santissima Villazzano, Trent, there is a shrine to the Divine Mercy with a life-size icon of the Divine Mercy Image.

On the fourth day of praying in front of this icon Ugo suddenly noticed the arms of the image stretched out to him and a tremendous warmth flowed through his body. He found himself standing on his feet with his arms outstretched to the Lord and he heard himself loudly praising Jesus the Divine Mercy. He saw Jesus coming down to him, his white garment blowing as if in a breeze, he thought, "My God, this is the man from Galilee coming towards me." He heard Jesus say in a clear voice, "Rise up and walk." He began to walk. All his ailments were at that instant cured and he was more physically perfect than he had ever been in his life. On August 19th 1990, Ugo returned to the Vatican and during a Papal Audience at Paul VI

Hall, was taken to meet John Paul II again. He told him about the great grace he had received and thanked him for the words of inspiration which led him to Trent which resulted in this great miracle of Divine Mercy. He gave John Paul a copy of the Divine Image, with the signatures on the back of the many people in the church who witnessed the miracle on that day. *This great moment is also recorded in a photo on the next page.*

I met Ugo and his spiritual director shortly after his miracle occurred in Trent. He invited me to his home in Vicenza where I stayed with him for a week. We kept in touch after that, and when I organised the speakers for first conference on Divine Mercy in 1992, I invited him as the main speaker. He visited me in Dublin on a number of occasions after that. Ugo went to work in Calcutta with Mother Teresa for number of years after his miraculous healing. When he was leaving she gave him her Rosary beads. He gave me this Rosary as the greatest gift he could give me just before he died. In his youth he had been a member of a Young Mafia Gang. His greatest ambition was to meet some of these old friends, (now men) but still associated with criminality and bring them to God. Unfortunately it seemed they did not appreciate this. He continued to try, but was found shot dead in a laneway a short time after his last effort.

Ugo thanks John Paul II

THE 1st MIRACLE AT THE TOMB OF SR. FAUSTINA

*"You will be the secretary to my Mercy
in this life and the next". (Diary 1605)*

Before the age of 15, Maureen Digan enjoyed a
normal healthy life. Then she was struck down
with a very serious, slowly progressive but
terminal disease called Lymphedima. This is a
disease that does not respond to medication
and does not go into remission. Within the next
ten years Maureen had 50 operations and had
lengthy confinements in Hospital of up to a
year at a time. Friends and relations suggested
she should pray and put her trust in God.
Maureen said she could not understand why
God had allowed her to get this disease in the
first place, and had lost her faith completely.
Eventually her deteriorating condition necessi-
tated the amputation of one leg. One evening
while Maureen was in hospital her husband
Bob went to a film called 'Divine Mercy No
Escape', and there he became convinced that if
Sr. Faustina needed miracles to become a Saint
perhaps his wife could be the first one. Bob per-
suaded Maureen and the Doctors that she
should go to the graveside of Sr. Faustina in
Poland. They arrived in Poland on March 23rd
1981 and Maureen went to confession for the first
time since she was a young girl. At the tomb of

In my heart I heard St. Faustina say "if you ask for my help, I will give it to you"

Saint Faustina, Maureen remembers saying *"O.K. Faustina I came a long way, now do something"*... In her heart she heard *"If you ask for my help, I will give it to you"*. Suddenly all the pain seemed to drain out of her body and her swollen leg which was due to be amputated, went back to its normal size. It was so traumatic, she thought she was having a nervous breakdown.

When she returned to the U.S.A. she was examined by five doctors who came to the conclusion that she was completely healed. They had no medical explanation for the sudden healing of this incurable disease. The accumulated evidence for this miracle was examined in again in consultation with independent doctors appointed to give a report to the Sacred Congregation for the causes of saints. Having passed this test it was examined by a team of theologians. The cure was accepted by all as a miracle caused by Sr. Faustina's intercession. Sr. Faustina was beatified on 18th April 1993.

APOSTLES OF MERCY PRAYER

Merciful Jesus, we believe in You,
and we trust in You.
Come to the aid of our weakness
and our incapacity.
Grant that we may be able to make
You known and loved by all
and confident in the
immensity of Your Love
we may be able to combat the evil
which is in us and in all the world,

for Your Glory and our salvation. Amen.

THE 2ND MIRACLE REQUIRED FOR SAINTHOOD WAS FATHER RONALD PYTEL

I was invited to the Agape Meal in the Vatican with John Paul II in 2000, for the canonisation of Saint Faustina. Here I met the main witness to the 2nd miracle, Cardiologist Professor Nicholas Fortuin, who was Fr. Pytel's cardiologist.

In a conversation with him, he explained he was the chief cardiologist in Johns Hopkins University Hospital, Baltimore, and lectured to students on cardiology; I felt the most striking thing he said was that he was not a believer.

He explained the reason he was here in Rome, it was that at his first examination of Fr. Pytel, he diagnosed that he was in profound heart failure and needed an urgent aortic valve replacement. Then some weeks later when he was preparing Fr.Pytel for this operation, he told me he was amazed to find he was looking at a heart so perfect it was like the heart of an eighteen year old.

To the many medical practioneers who were examining the cause for canonisation, this was his witness. His assistants at the hospital also gave witness to this extraordinary finding.

He told me, regardless of his own lack of faith, he would in future lectures, be telling students that they could consider faith as a factor in healing. Fr. Ron Pytel the recipient of the miracle was also at this Agape Meal.

His story began in 1995 when he was forty eight years old. He was spiritual director of a prayer group, 'the Baltimore Healing Ministry'.

Because of his heart condition, he had resigned himself to an early death. His heart was so damaged that a short walk left him exhausted. His weight was down to eight stone. His quality of life was low. Fr. Pytel of the Holy Rosary Catholic Church, in Baltimore, was a great promoter of the message of Divine Mercy, and had been devoted to Saint Faustina and Divine Mercy for many years.

In June 1995, Father Pytel went to cardiologist Nicholas Fortuin, a professor of cardiology at Johns Hopkins University Hospital. Dr. Fortuin told Fr. Pytel that he was in profound heart failure.

He arranged for Fr. Pytel to undergo an immediate operation for an aortic valve replacement under his guidance, with the best surgeons at Johns Hopkins Hospital. Professor Fortuin told him that even if the operation was a complete success he could never return to an active life.

Some weeks later Fr. Pytel's prayer group were praying to St. Faustina for at least an improvement in his health, during this prayer Father Pytel collapsed and fell to the floor, he recalls he could not move a muscle. *"It was as though I was paralysed."* His prayer group knelt around him thinking he was dying, they implored St. Faustina to save him. After fifteen minutes unconscious on the floor, he recovered and he felt so good he could hardly believe it.

Although Fr. Pytel felt better immediately afterward, he did not know that his heart had been fully healed until his check-up. Medical experts have concluded that Father Pytel's

heart recovery was so extraordinary that it could only be the result of divine intervention.

The Agape Meal was in celebration of the canonisation of Saint Faustina and this extraordinary healing was the miracle that was instrumental in her canonisation.

Fr. Ron Pytel

BECOME AN APOSTLE OF DIVINE MERCY
and help Jesus save souls

What is an Apostle of Divine Mercy

APOSTLE - from the Greek meaning one who is sent or messenger

of DIVINE - meaning, of God

MERCY - or misericordia in latin, is made up of three smaller words

Miseris, meaning miserable

Cor, meaning heart or love

Dare, meaning to give

So an *Apostle of Divine Mercy* is one who *brings God's love to the miserable. For no one that is aware of God's existence and love could be miserable. Unfortunately this world is full of miserable people.*

All Catholics *are called to be Apostles and participate in extending the Kingdom of Christ throughout the world for the greater glory of God the Father and to direct the whole Universe to Christ. (Apostolicam Actuositatem 2).*

(Vatican 2, decree of the Apostolate of the Laity 18th November, 1965.)

CAN YOU BE A MESSENGER
OF GOD'S MERCY?

God usually chooses the weakest and simplest souls as tools for his greatest works; this we can see when we look at the first men he chose to be his Apostles, or when we look at the history of the Church and see what great works were done by souls that were least capable of accomplishing them: for it is in this way that God's works are revealed for what they are, **the works of God.**

(from the Diary of Blessed Michael Sopocko)

"Act in such a way that all those who come in contact with you go away joyful. Sow happiness about you because you have received much from God. Give generously (of yourself) to others, they should take leave of you, with hearts full of joy."

(from the Diary of Saint Faustina)

Jesus said: **As often as you wish to make Me happy, speak to the world about My great and unfathomable Mercy.** *(Diary 164)*

I do not reward for good results but for patience and hardship undergone for My sake. *(Diary 86)*

Do all you possibly can for this work of My Mercy - I am giving mankind the final hope for salvation, that is recourse to My Mercy. *(Diary 998)*

In the old covenant I sent prophets wielding thunderbolts - today I am sending you with My mercy. Before the day of justice, I am sending the day of mercy. *(Diary 1588)*

FAMILY ENTHRONEMENT OF THE DIVINE MERCY IMAGE IN THE HOME

The image of Divine Mercy is a source of endless graces for all the family. Place it in your own home and let it be a means to re-invigorate belief and protect your family. The image should be exposed in a position where it can be seen by all who dwell in the house as they go about their daily life.

Jesus said to Faustina: **"I am offering people a vessel to which they are to keep coming for graces"**. The vessel is this image with the signature "Jesus I Trust in you". (*Diary 327*)

Family Act of Consecration:

We consecrate our entire life from here on to you without reserve. Into Your hands we abandon our past, our present, our future. Jesus, we ask You, from this day on, to look after this family. Help us to be true children of God and children of Your Blessed Mother, Mary.

Through this image may Your Divine Mercy triumph over all the powers of evil the world over. May all who venerate it never perish. May it be their joy in life, their hope in death and their glory in eternity.

This we ask through Christ Our Lord, Amen.

I dedicate this book to Jesus the Divine Mercy whose image changed my life forever on a day in February 1981.

To Fr. Berchmans Walsh O.C.S.O. whose memory I honour here, he was the inspiration I needed to put this book together on a day in February 1985.

To Our Lady who, on a day in April 1987 asked me never to give up this important work of spreading this urgent message of Her Son's Divine Mercy.

Nearly five million copies of this book have now been sold throughout the world. All proceeds from this book go entirely to our Divine Mercy Apostolate, to help spread His mercy, in deed word and prayer.

The deeds are carried out by our Charity:

"HELP US DRY THE TEARS"

The title for the Charity comes from the Diary of Saint Faustina, where she said, *"Once, a pain pierced my soul, and I began to pray this way: "Most merciful Jesus, I beseech You through the intercession of Your Saints, and especially the inter- cession of Your dearest Mother who nurtured You from childhood, I beg You, Jesus, look not on our sins, but on the tears of little children, on the hunger and the cold they suffer. Jesus for the sake of these innocent ones, grant me the grace that I am asking of You. At that moment, I saw the Lord Jesus, (His eyes filled with tears) and He said to me,* **You see, My daughter, what great compassion I have for them, (the suffering children) Know that it is they who uphold this whole world."** *(Diary 286).*

Jesus cries out for mercy for these pitiful children, and we who have received His message must respond, not just with words but also with works. When you buy this book you are now taking part in helping us with our work, helping to save lives, as well as souls. I have been promoting this message since 1981, and this is what I believe Jesus meant when He said "bring My mercy to the world, in deed, word, and prayer." *(Diary 742).*   *Val Conlon*

Abandoned Baby in Romania

"HELP US DRY THE TEARS FOUNDATION"
"DIVINE MERCY IN ACTION"

Romania and Moldova in 1989 became known in the world as the land of orphans and abandoned children since. Still for some years after, the world was doing very little about it. When I went to see for my Charity I saw many pitiful sights, I saw children living in dormitories which were icy cold in summer I shuddered to think what the dormitories would be like in winter, with no heating. But the most frightening thing I experienced there was the silence. If you put hundreds of children into a building together, the first thing you expect to hear when you go in, is a constant din of noise, but as I walked the corridors all I could hear was the echo of my own footsteps, on the cold stone floors. I wondered what induced this terrible silence. Poverty of material things was not the worst poverty I saw, but the stark poverty of emotion, children with blank expressions on their faces, resigned to a life of misery, a life without love, a life without hope.

But this was not the worst I was to see, when I went to Bucharest I wasn't prepared for what I saw there, not far from a Government building, I saw a filthy young emaciated child coming up out of a sewer holding a soggy bit of bread in her hand. As she climbed up out of the sewer, six other little children followed in the same condition. These are huge large sewers with paths & hot pipes for the city buildings running through them. I saw these children as young as seven or eight years of age, moving like zombies, filthy dirty and high on glue. They were what's known as the street children. The glue numbed their minds and helped them endure the conditions they lived in and the hunger they were experiencing. During the winter, which goes below minus ten degrees, a lot of these children die from exposure, others will die of disease and malnutrition, as they go deeper into the sewers, to find the only warmth they can.

Jesus said, **"I demand from you deeds of mercy, you must not shrink from this or try to excuse or absolve yourself from it. I give you three ways of exercising mercy, the FIRST BY DEED, the second by word, and the third by prayer."** *(Diary of St. Faustina 742)* - This was a report by Val Conlon to his HUDT Charity after his first visit to Romania in 1998.

A short time after, our foundation opened a number of houses in Eastern Europe. In these houses we employed religious sisters and trained nurses to help bring God's Divine Mercy to these destitute children. The children were given medical aid, food, clothing, education, but most of all they were given love.

**To Make a Donation Call us 01 8491458
or 00353 1 8491458 from outside Ireland
Send cheque by POST to
"HELP US DRY THE TEARS" (IRELAND)
Maryville, Skerries, Co. Dublin, Ireland, K34NW54**

**Please make cheque payable to:
"Help Us Dry The Tears"
Help us Dry the Tears Foundation is a
Registered Charity No. CHY14320**

With grateful thanks to the Marian priests and Brothers who through the Association of Marian Helpers, Stockbridge Mass. gave me great help with my Apostolate work on a day in 1987 when they gave me permission to copy their English translation of the diary of Sister Faustina.

With grateful thanks to Saint Faustina's order, "The Congregation of our Lady of Mercy" for permission to publish from their books on Divine Mercy in English and Spanish.

Both these permissions help us to do our work of mercy with the suffering children of the third world in our

"HELP US DRY THE TEARS" FOUNDATION

Love of God and love of one's brothers and sisters are inseparable. By this we know that when we love the children of God, we love God, and obey His commandments. *(John Chap 5 : Verse 2)*

Please Visit Divine Mercy in Action
www.hudt.org